DEVELOP
RELENTLESS
COMPETITORS
DRILLBOOK

ADDITIONAL RESOURCES BY JEFF JANSSEN

BOOKS

How to Develop Relentless Competitors: A Proven 5-Step Process to Transform Your Passive Athletes into Fierce Competitors

The Team Captain's Leadership Manual: The Complete Guide to Developing Team Leaders Whom Coaches Respect and Teammates Trust

Championship Team Building: What Every Coach Needs to Know to Build a Motivated, Committed, and Cohesive Team

Jeff Janssen's Peak Performance Playbook: 50 Drills, Activities, and Ideas to Inspire Your Team, Build Mental Toughness, and Improve Team Chemistry

The Seven Secrets of Successful Coaches: How to Unlock and Unleash Your Team's Full Potential

The Mental Makings of Champions Workbook: How to Win the Mental Game

All resources can be ordered at www.jeffjanssen.com

WEBSITES

www.ChampionshipCoachesNetwork.com

www.TeamCaptainsNetwork.com

DEVELOP RELENTLESS COMPETITORS DRILLBOOK

75 Proven Drills, Activities, and Ideas to Bring Out the Fierce Competitor in Your Athletes

JEFF JANSSEN, M.S.

Published by Winning The Mental Game
6841 Piershill Lane, Cary, NC 27519
Phone: 1-888-721-TEAM
Fax: (919) 303-4338
Email: jeff@jeffjanssen.com
Website: www.jeffjanssen.com

Library of Congress Control Number: 2010933553

ISBN 978-1-8928827-5-2

Published in the United States of America

10 9 8 7 6 5 4 3 2 1

DEDICATION

To my two terrific children, Ryan and Jillian
I love you and your competitiveness. Use it for good to make
the world a better place.

TABLE OF CONTENTS

INTRODUCTION   **1**

SECTION 1: Relentless Competitor Drills For All Sports   **5**

    1.   O'B OLYMPICS   **6**

    2.   ILLINI GAMES   **7**

    3.   WATER BALANCE   **9**

    4.   PUPPET SUMO   **11**

    5.   STICK JOUSTING   **12**

    6.   BALANCE CHALLENGE   **13**

    7.   HIGH STANDARDS DRILLS   **14**

    8.   DISADVANTAGE DRILLS   **15**

SECTION 2: Relentless Competitor Concepts For All Sports   **17**

    9.   CAROLINA BASKETBALL'S AWARDS BOARD   **18**

    10. URBAN MEYER'S CHAMPION'S CLUB   **20**

    11. NOTRE DAME'S COMPETE AGAINST THE BEST STATS
OF THE PROGRAM   **21**

    12. ANSON DORRANCE'S COMPETITIVE MATRIX   **22**

    13. PITT'S BATTLE OF THE PANTHERS   **23**

    14. TEXAS FOOTBALL'S DEDICATION DAY   **24**

    15. DUKE BASKETBALL'S SLAP THE FLOOR DEFENSE   **25**

    16. COACH DAN GABLE'S ACCOUNTABILITY TEST   **26**

    17. MATCH PLAY AND BOARD GAME CHALLENGE   **27**

    18. GPA CHALLENGE   **28**

    19. HOUSES   **29**

    20. NAILS AWARD FOR COMPETITIVENESS   **30**

    21. CREATE CHALLENGE LADDERS   **31**

22. WIN THE WARM-UP   **32**

23. TRAINING WITH BIGGER, STRONGER, AND FASTER COMPETITION   **33**

SECTION 3: Relentless Competitor Activities For All Sports   **35**

24. TOP COMPETITORS LIST   **36**

25. CLASSY VS. CRASS COMPETITOR   **37**

26. WARRIOR NICKNAMES   **38**

27. COMPETITIVENESS CONTINUUM™ DISCUSSION   **39**

28. RATE YOUR TEAMMATES ON THE COMPETITIVENESS CONTINUUM™   **41**

29. DOMINATE YOUR TERRITORY   **42**

30. PRIZED POSSESSION: WHAT'S WORTH FIGHTING FOR?   **43**

31. MOTIVATIONAL MOVIES   **44**

32. MOTIVATIONAL THEMES   **45**

33. POST-GAME COMPETITON ANALYSIS   **46**

34. 20 POST-COMPETITION COMPETITIVENESS QUESTIONS   **47**

SECTION 4: Relentless Competitor Stories For All Sports   **49**

35. OLD COACH AND THE LAKE STORY   **50**

36. BURN THE BOATS STORY   **51**

37. STEEL MILL STORY   **52**

38. THE BIKE STORY   **53**

39. GILA MONSTER ANALOGY   **54**

40. FINDING WAYS TO WIN WITH TWO KINDS OF COMPETITORS   **55**

41. THE CRYING SCOUT TEAM PLAYER STORY   **56**

42. LION AND GAZELLE STORY   **57**

43. FROM PASSIVE FRESHMAN TO COMPETITIVE NATIONAL TEAM CAPTAIN   **58**

44. MOM AND BABY STORY   **59**

SECTION 5: Relentless Competitor Drills For Strength And Conditioning — 61

45. WILDCAT GAMES — 62

46. MONSTER GATORS — 64

47. ANSON DORRANCE'S SPEED LADDER — 65

48. SUPERMAN PUSH-UPS — 66

49. RUNNING AS A REWARD—POSITIVE CONDITIONING — 67

50. NEGATIVE SPLIT — 68

SECTION 6: Relentless Competitor Drills For Basketball — 71

51. THREE STOPS AND OUT — 72

52. MASTER OF THE BOARDS—MICHIGAN STATE REBOUNDING DRILL — 73

53. FOUR ON FOUR DEFENSIVE CUT THROAT — 74

54. SIDELINE PASSING — 75

55. GUT CHECK DRILL — 76

SECTION 7: Relentless Competitor Drills For Soccer — 79

56. 4 v 4 + 2 GAME — 80

57. DAWG BOWL — 82

58. ATTITUDE TRAINING — 83

59. 3 v 2 + GK's — 84

60. DEAL WITH IT — 85

SECTION 8: Relentless Competitor Drills For Volleyball — 89

61. COMPENSATION — 90

62. TWO-MINUTE DRILL — 91

63. TIMED RAGE — 92

64. YOU THE MAN — 93

65. HITTER VS. HITTER — 94

SECTION 9: Relentless Competitor Drills For Softball/Baseball   97

    66. COMPETITIVE BULLPENS   **98**

    67. 4 CORNER 3 IN A ROW   **100**

    68. STAY ALIVE   **101**

    69. WALL TO WALL SOFTBALL   **103**

    70. THE QUICK PITCH BUNTING DRILL   **104**

SECTION 10: Relentless Competitor Drills for Football   107

    71. COACH JERRY KILL'S WARRIOR ELITE PROGRAM   **108**

    72. COACH PETE CARROLL'S COMPETITION TUESDAYS   **110**

    73. BERMUDA TRIANGLE   **111**

    74. DETERMINATION   **112**

    75. SWISS BALL SUMO   **113**

NOTES   **114**

PHOTO CREDITS   **114**

ABOUT THE AUTHOR   **116**

ACKNOWLEDGMENTS

A HUGE thank you to Erin Lindsey who did a spectacular job in helping me compile all the drills. Thank you to Twila Kaufman who assisted with the soccer drills. I also appreciate the editing help of Jackie Fain and Mike McNeill.

Special thank you to the people who kindly contributed or inspired the ideas in this book including: Tim O'Brien, Steve Oldenburg, Jeffrey Pierce, Scott Ditter, Craig Kennedy, Jodie Collins, Roy Williams, Jerod Haase, Urban Meyer, Deanna Gumpf, Anson Dorrance, Penny Semaia, Abbi Terveer, Mack Brown, Mike Krzyzewski, Jerry Kill, Kristina Therriault, Dan Gable, Wes Bruns, Renee Slone, Matt Giufre, Dean Lockwood, Pat Summitt, Gary Barnett, Carla Overbeck, Christopher Zorich, Marc Hill, Kate Costanzo, Terry Wilson, Molly Grisham, Lance Harter, Tom Izzo, Waleed Samaha, Rich Hoyt, Joe Sagula, Jason Allen, Rey Bechard, Tracey Kornau, Shannon Ellis, Rich Maloney, Karen Linder, Scott Chausse, Mike Truncale, Paul O'Brien, Pete Carroll, Shelley Johnson, Eric Gobble, Jerome Learman, and Tim Kuhn.

INTRODUCTION

Welcome to the *Develop Relentless Competitors Drillbook*. This one of a kind *Drillbook* provides you with 75 different drills, activities, stories, and ideas to help you transform your passive, wimpy, and entitled athletes into the focused and fierce competitors you need to succeed.

The *Drillbook* reinforces and extends the competitive strategies, models, and concepts shared in the companion *How to Develop Relentless Competitors* book. It also provides you with a wealth of practical and proven ideas that you can implement as soon as today's practice.

In addition to containing the drills, activities, and stories I use to develop Competitors at several of the nation's top colleges, many of the competitive drills in this book have been contributed by fellow college and high school coaches across the country. So these competitive drills are time-tested and represent the best drills and activities available to develop relentless Competitors.

The first part of the *Develop Relentless Competitors Drillbook* includes a variety of drills and concepts that can be used or adapted by virtually any sport. You'll learn the inside strategies used to develop intense Competitors by top coaches at North Carolina, Duke, Texas, Florida, Tennessee, Michigan, Illinois, Arizona, and Notre Dame. The drills, ideas, and stories listed have contributed to National Championships and Final Four appearances across a variety of sports.

There's also a dedicated section for competitive drills and ideas for strength and conditioning; as a big part of a strength coach's job is to develop mental toughness and competitiveness in addition to physical strength and endurance. Finally, the last section includes drills that are sport specific for basketball, soccer, football, volleyball, and baseball/softball. By the end, I hope you will see there are literally dozens of ways you can make your practices and athletes more competitive.

Remember, the more you make your practices competitive, the more your athletes will learn how to compete. The great thing about sports is that you can easily make almost any drill competitive. Simply keep score, monitor the time, measure the distance, etc. and announce and/or post the results to see if your athletes can continually improve.

When using the drills and ideas in your practices, be sure to invest the time to discuss the 5-phase competitive response model discussed in the *How to Develop Relentless Competitors* book with your athletes:

1. Declare War

2. Ready

3. Aim

4. Fire

5. Fight to the Finish

This model provides them with the solid framework they need to initiate and sustain the competitive response. Take the time to also monitor your athletes' competitive response in terms of their purpose, power, preparation, precision, and persistence as it relates to the Missile Strike analogy relayed in the book.

While you have dozens of competitive options in this *Drillbook*, remember too that not every drill should be competitive. When your athletes are first learning new strategies and techniques or refining their skills, you need to provide them with an opportunity to experience and practice the skill in a low-pressure environment, rather than worrying about the outcome. But once the skills and strategies are fully understood and somewhat automatic, you can then make your drills competitive.

I hope you and your athletes get a lot out of this *Drillbook*. Please contact me at jeff@ jeffjanssen.com for any comments you might have. Also, I encourage you to submit any additional drills, activities, stories, or ideas you might have to develop athletes into better Competitors. We might be able to include them in future editions of the book. Thank you!

JEFF JANSSEN,
Founder, Janssen Sports Leadership Center

RELENTLESS COMPETITOR DRILLS FOR ALL SPORTS

1. O'B Olympics

2. Illini Games

3. Water Balance

4. Puppet Sumo

5. Stick Jousting

6. Balance Challenge

7. High Standards Drills

8. Disadvantage Drills

1. O'B OLYMPICS

Objective
Promote competitive spirit and teamwork.

Directions
The O'B Olympics can be adapted to any situation and can be used at any time in any season. We make up a tour of our campus which includes any number of stops at stations where different challenges must be met. They may be endurance challenges like a 2-mile run. They can be strength tests like throwing a medicine ball for distance. They can be grueling challenges like weighted sled pulls for time or skill-oriented like hitting targets with throws. Tire throws, mini-game scores, hill climbing times, tonnage lifted in timed exercises, and any number of other challenges can be created.

The competition can be run with teams or individually. It can be done on one day or over a several day Olympiad. It can even be done in stages over the course of the season with standings posted and handicapping commentary included.

To provide incentive, you can play for field work duties or other chores like cleaning up the locker room, carrying the winners' bags, etc. We release our winners from field work for a day or a week. Other types of prizes can be awarded, or as in our situation, the losers buy the winners a huge dinner out on the town.

Discussion
The O'B Olympics can involve "strategizing" among teams and maximizing the talents of all team members. The cooperative efforts can be tremendous for a team. For even greater team benefits, include players in the design of the games and watch what they create for themselves! Let the Olympics begin!

Contributed by:
Tim O'Brien, Assistant Baseball Coach, University of Maryland, Baltimore County

2. ILLINI GAMES

Objective

The goal behind the Illini games is to have female athletes participate and enjoy active, competitive environments outside of their current sport. Over the past several years at Illinois, I noticed that female athletes in the off-season rarely perform competitive physical activities outside their own sport. In contrast, male athletes tend to perform competitive activities such as pick-up basketball, Ultimate Frisbee, football, etc. in their leisure time.

Directions

The first year I put the Illini games together it was met with a little resistance, but some athletes decided to humor me and give it a try. The first game we played was Ultimate Frisbee. We had two fields going of 8 vs. 8 playing 15 minute games. During the games, the athletes were hooting and hollering and having a great time, while also getting in a pretty good workout.

After each game I had about 75% of the athletes asking if we were done and if they could leave. I would simply say, "It looks like you're having a great time out there why would you want to go"? Their response was always, "We are having a great time, but . . ." and would continue with whatever excuse in the book. Most of the time I or other athletes would convince enough people to stay and play. Over time more athletes from various teams joined in and attitudes changed about the Illini Games. Instead of it being viewed as a workout session, the Illini Games have turned into a weekly event where even former Illini stop in to play.

Games Played:

- Ultimate Frisbee
- Ultimate Football
- Castle (A mixture of tag and capture the flag)—(Illini Games Favorite)
- Ultimate Hand Ball (on roller hockey venue)
- Power Ball (Short Court Tennis w/Medicine Ball)
- Speed Ball (Sand Volleyball Court)
- Flag Tag
- I'm also trying to put together a team relay triathlon.

A lot of games are played what we call "Ultimate" to even the playing field across the different sports and abilities as well as increase physical activity. "Ultimate" in Ultimate Football means there is no stoppage of play, you can only take two steps after you catch the ball. If the ball hits the ground, it is a turnover—as possession switches to the defense. The on-ball defender can count to 5 Mississippi to cause a turnover. This allows athletes who are not in as cardiovascular shape (volleyball/softball compared to soccer) to compete on a more even playing field.

I feel that the Illini Games have really helped bring out competitiveness in athletes that do not have physical contact in their sport such as volleyball, swimming and diving, and softball.

Contributed by:

Steve Oldenburg, University of Illinois Strength and Conditioning Staff

3. WATER BALANCE

Objective
Water Balance is a great drill that promotes competitiveness, teamwork, and leadership.

Set Up
- ❏ Large plastic buckets the kind used for putting drinks and ice in at a picnic— similar looking to the old tin wash tubs. You will need one bucket per every 4-5 players on your team.

- ❏ Access to a water supply (hose or pump)

- ❏ Stop Watch

Divide players into two teams of 4 or 5. Fill the plastic buckets at least half full with water (the more water, the more difficult the game). Have each team join hands and make a circle. Then have them lie on their backs with their legs up in the air, with their bottoms facing the center of the circle. Have them move together as close as possible so that their bottoms are as tight to the center of the circle as possible. With their backs on the ground and their legs in the air they should resemble a pedestal table with no top.

Directions
Once they are in this position, the water filled plastic bucket should be positioned atop their feet. The players should be able to support and balance the weight without an issue. Once both teams are balancing and supporting the water bucket, a series of commands will be given, that each team has to complete within a 1 minute time frame. The commands will continue to be given until the water bucket is dropped or failure to complete the command within the 1 minute time frame occurs, which will constitute a loss for the team as well as a drenching.

Commands
1. Two people each remove one shoe.

2. Remaining people remove one shoe from another person other than yourself.

3. One person put shoe back on (typically this gets tricky because when the shoe was removed it was not put nearby where it is reachable).

4. One more person put shoe back on.

5. One more person put shoe back on.

6. One more person put shoe back on.

7. One more person put shoe back on (if you have 5 on a team).

8. If play is still continuing at this point, start to have individuals remove one foot from balancing until you are down to only 2 feet balancing the bucket.

Of course you can make up your own commands as well.

9. The winning team is the one that is successfully able to execute all the commands without spilling the water.

Discussion
Discuss the leadership and teamwork of the people in your group.
Who was the most competitive person in each group?
How competitive was each group?

Contributed by:
Jeffrey S. Pierce, North Oldham Mustangs, Softball Coach

4. PUPPET SUMO

Objective

This activity is not only a great competitive drill; it works on balance, strength and focus.

Set Up

❏ Make a ring 5 feet in diameter (use paint on the grass or tape on the gym floor).

❏ You will need two towels.

Directions

Have two competitors step into the ring.

The competitors each grab the opposite ends of two towels, one in each hand, so that the two towels connect them, holding the ends in their hands.

On the coach's signal, the object of the drill is to get your opponent out of the ring by stepping on or over the line or letting go of the towel.

The only rule is that you cannot push your opponent.

The rest of the team chooses a person to cheer for. Losing side does push ups, up-downs or "Burpies."

Variations

Can make variations by having a time limit or putting a line across the circle to make the area smaller.

Can also create a tournament where the winner advances on to the next round.

Contributed by:

Scott Ditter, Selah High School, Assistant Coach

5. STICK JOUSTING

Objective

The purpose of stick jousting is to create a one on one environment that promotes competitiveness.

Set Up

❏ In stick jousting, we use the center circle for basketball (obviously any circle will do) and a broomstick, or something similar with the ends padded. I cover the ends with pieces of a pool noodle.

Directions

The two combatants face each other and grasp the stick. The stick is parallel to the ground. On the coach's signal, the challenge of the drill is to push the other person out of the circle. Twisting the stick is not allowed.

One great contest between two upper classmen went on for 11 minutes as neither would give up. This activity is done on a challenge basis with weight classes and with a challenge board. The one on one nature and close proximity lends itself to a real increase in a person's competitive nature.

I found Stick Jousting to be very effective. I remember when I had two little girls in the second grade (wearing their dresses). When I said "Go," they started to push and all of a sudden their level of competitiveness just took off.

Contributed by:

Craig Kennedy, Assistant Coach, Troy Women's Basketball

6. BALANCE CHALLENGE

Objective

This drill is a great one for teaching your athletes that competitiveness needs to be a balance between being both intense and intelligent.

Directions

Have your athletes partner up with a person roughly equal in size to start. The partners should face each other standing about three feet away. Have each person in the pair raise their hands so their palms are slightly in front of their chest and open toward their partner—as if they are catching a pass, feet should be parallel about shoulder width apart.

Once they are in this position, the goal of the activity is to get their partner off balance by either:

1. Hitting their partner's hands with their open palms in an effort to knock them backwards or off balance.

2. Dodging or deflecting their partner's hand thrusts so that their partner loses their balance by falling forward or sideways. (Athletes can quickly move their hands to the side or down when a partner tries to strike them—causing the partner to miss and fall forward.)

As soon as one person loses their balance by taking any kind of step with either of their feet, they lose the activity.

The winner moves on to challenge another winner in the group, and the losers must then cheer loudly for the person who beat them throughout the rest of the competition. The activity continues until two people remain in the Balance Challenge. The final winner is the last person standing.

Discussion

After the activity, you can ask your athletes the following questions:

■ What tactics did you take to try to win the competition?

■ How did intensity and intelligence play a role in the activity?

■ What did you learn about competitiveness, balance, and composure through this activity?

■ What can we learn from the last two people who made it to the finals of the competition?

■ How can we gain from this activity in becoming a better Competitor?

Contributed by:

Jodie Collins of Me to We www.metowe.com

7. HIGH STANDARDS DRILLS

High Standards Drills can be set up with most any kind of physical drill. The key concept is to establish a specific high standard of performance that your athletes must achieve or surpass before they can complete the drill.

For example, some baseball coaches do a drill called 27 outs. The coach calls out various situations and the defense must make 27 consecutive error-free plays before the drill is complete. The 27 outs symbolizes the total number of outs needed to win a game (9 innings x 3 outs = 27 outs. Softball coaches can easily use 21 outs for 7 innings of play.) If an error is made or the person throws to the wrong base, the count starts over at zero.

High Standards Drills can be set up by making a specified number of consecutive plays in a row. Or they can be set up by achieving a certain number of successes in a specific period of time.

Some basketball coaches require their athletes to make a certain number of layups in a specified period of time (see the Sideline Passing Drill in the basketball section of this book). If the team achieves or surpasses the goal, the drill is over. If they fall short, they must keep doing the drill until they achieve the standard. Obviously the drill typically becomes tougher over time as the athletes get more and more tired.

Not only will you see Competitors emerge when you do these drills because they want to get them over and done, you will also see leaders attempt to step up, motivate, and refocus the team.

The potential drawback with High Standards Drills is there might be times when your athletes fail to meet the standard after numerous attempts, or take an unusually long time to do so. You must plan your practices accordingly when using High Standards Drills because it is hard to predict how long it will take your team to reach the standard. Thus, be sure your standards are also realistic in addition to challenging. You can always raise the standard as the season goes on.

Athletes can even create their own set of high standards drills. I remember a basketball player at Marquette named Jim McIlvaine, who made a pact with himself to never leave practice until he hit 10 consecutive free throws. Sometimes McIlvaine was done on his first try, but other times he was there an hour afterwards until he made 10 in a row. Whether for individuals or teams, High Standards Drills are great for developing commitment, confidence, and competitiveness.

8. DISADVANTAGE DRILLS

Disadvantage drills are an effective way to build the competitiveness and confidence of your athletes. They involve putting your athletes at a competitive disadvantage by altering the rules of the game to see how your team responds. Some examples include:

- Having your quarterback try to complete passes against an extra defender.

- Having your baseball or softball hitters start with an 0-2 count.

- Having your basketball team break a press against 6 defenders—or not allowing them to dribble when advancing the ball up the court.

- Allowing your tennis players only a single serve instead of two before faulting.

- Having your soccer players try to score on a smaller than regulation size goal.

Disadvantage drills force your athletes to focus and compete with more intelligence and intensity to get the job done. Yes, because of the contrived disadvantage they will likely experience a good deal of failure in your practice settings. But by learning how to succeed in these extra difficult environments, they will get an extra boost of confidence when it comes time to playing the real game without the disadvantages in place.

By making your practices more difficult than your actual competitions, you develop a certain mentality and mental toughness in your athletes that hardens and prepares them for any challenge an opponent might throw their way.

SECTION 2

RELENTLESS COMPETITOR CONCEPTS FOR ALL SPORTS

9. North Carolina Basketball's Awards Board

10. Urban Meyer's Champions Club

11. Notre Dame's Compete Against the Program's Best Stats

12. Anson Dorrance's Competitive Matrix

13. Pitt's Battle of the Panthers

14. Texas Football's Dedication Day

15. Duke Basketball's Slap the Floor Defense

16. Coach Dan Gable's Accountability Test

17. Match Play and Board Game and Challenge

18. GPA Challenge

19. Houses

20. Nails Award Voted on by the Team

21. Challenge Ladders

22. Win the Warm-up

23. Training with Bigger, Stronger, and Faster Competition

9. CAROLINA BASKETBALL'S AWARDS BOARD

How can you get your players to compete hard all the time?

Coach Roy Williams and the Carolina men's basketball program uses a unique charting system for practices and games that focuses on all the little things that need to be done to create a winning team. Carolina meticulously tracks and rewards players for their efforts and results on EVERY possession on both ends of the court.

The charting system and accompanying Awards Board helps the players focus on the key processes of being successful and rewards those players who consistently compete and contribute in a multitude of subtle yet important ways to the team's success.

Charting the Team's Progress

Usually within hours after the game, the entire staff sits down together to watch the film of the game to examine each offensive and defensive possession in great detail. Defensively they record charges taken, deflections, boxouts, close outs, and a whole host of 37 subtle, yet important categories.

Offensively they record the quality of screens a player sets, the times a player loses the ball even when he doesn't turn it over, and a tally of passes that would have been assists had the player made the shot or was not fouled.

All of these in-depth stats create a ratio of positive plays to negative plays. This ratio is also one of the categories that Carolina uses to provide feedback to their players.

The players are given the information at the next team meeting following the game. As assistant coach Jerod Haase said, "When we have a 9:00 pm game during the ACC tournament, sometimes we are up until 3:00 or 4:00 in the morning grading the tape, so the players have the feedback the next morning at the team breakfast."

Coach Williams wants the players to have the feedback when the game is still fresh in their minds. He fondly remembers a teacher he once had who always had the tests graded for them the next day of class—all in an effort to help the students effectively learn the material. He, too, feels he owes it to his players to provide them with timely feedback.

Coach Williams reads off the names of the players who were the winners for each of the categories. Their names are then listed on the Awards Board that is positioned right outside the locker room door in the Smith Center. Not only do the winners of each category get acknowledged on the Awards Board, they also earn Plus Points, which can be used to get out of sprints at the end of practice.

In talking with the Carolina coaches and players, they cite five primary benefits of the charting system and Awards board.

1. Emphasizes the process of winning. The system focuses the players on the process rather than the outcome of winning. The primary emphasis is on doing all the little things that make the outcome and winning much more likely to happen.

2. Pride for winning category. Players take great pride in winning categories and seeing their names up on the board. It serves as a great incentive system for them to compete hard, especially when they can also get out of sprints at the end of practice.

3. Appreciates all the roles. The charting system allows role players to get more attention and positive strokes for the key things they bring to the team. While the stars receive the accolades for the glamorous stats like points and rebounding, the role players get their due on the Awards Board for doing all the necessary dirty work like setting screens, taking charges, and diving on the floor for loose balls.

4. Credibility of coaching staff enhanced. The credibility of the coaching staff is enhanced because the players see the coaches are serious about and committed to the process of winning. They are willing to dedicate the time (sometimes in the wee hours of the morning) to meticulously break down film and provide the players with key and timely feedback.

5. More objective criteria when playing time is questioned. Finally, the charting system quantifies a player's contribution on the court in a more objective way. If someone has a dispute about playing time, the numbers are a great resource to help a player see why he isn't playing, and what specifically he needs to do to earn more time.

The charting system and Awards Board has several benefits. It is something I encourage you to think about adapting and adopting with your program. Think about it . . . What seemingly little, yet massively important subtle stats are you charting and rewarding for your team?

Sit down with your coaching staff and make a list of all the little things you need your athletes to do that the casual fan might miss, but are vitally important to your team's success. Talk about their importance with your athletes and let them know your staff/managers will be recording them in their upcoming competitions. You too can create an Awards Board to acknowledge and reward the winners of each category. It is a simple yet effective thing you can do to reward the behaviors you want to see repeated. And it is an effective way to encourage your players to go hard on EVERY possession. Remember, that which gets recorded and rewarded often gets done, and done well.

10. URBAN MEYER'S CHAMPION'S CLUB

Florida football coach Urban Meyer has devised an incentive program for his team to enhance competitiveness, commitment, and character called the Champion's Club.

Athletes earn membership to the Champion's Club based on their effort on the field, attending class, and displaying exemplary off field behavior. The players who do the right thing are lavished with praise and the best Nike gear. Four times throughout the year, the players who make Champion's Club status are also treated to a banquet where they are served prime rib on linen tablecloths and eat off fine china for their efforts.

The athletes who do not achieve Champion's Club status don't get nice gear and must wear the hand me downs from year's past. At the banquet, they get hot dogs and half-cooked burgers with stale buns. They eat off plastic plates while sitting on splintered picnic tables. Finally, they must clear the dishes for those in the Champion's Club.

Coach Meyer says, "We try to reward achievement. There is no fairness at the University of Florida. We wanted to reward players who live right."

Out of 85 scholarship athletes and over 15 walk-ons, roughly 50 athletes earn Champion's Club status each quarter. You too can create your own Champion's Club for the athletes who represent your program with class and distinction. It is definitely an honor worth competing for with all the associated benefits.

Another idea that Coach Meyer uses to build competitiveness is to place a black stripe on all the freshmen players' helmets. The stripe is removed once the player does something that contributes significantly to the team. Removing the stripe means that the player has officially become a Gator.

Linebacker Brandon Spikes said, "It means a lot to me, meaning that I'll be a Gator very soon. That's one of the reasons I come to practice and work hard every day, trying to get my stripe off so I can be a Gator."

When players get their black stripe removed, an upperclassman on the team who serves as the player's "big brother" gives a speech on what his "little brother" did to earn the right to be a Gator. The freshman also stands and talks about what it means to be a Gator. Some of the players get quite emotional when it comes time to talking about officially being a Gator.

"We're trying to develop some tradition where that means a lot to people. The speeches where they remove the stripe have been fantastic," says Coach Meyer.

11. NOTRE DAME'S COMPETE AGAINST THE BEST STATS OF THE PROGRAM

Notre Dame softball coach Deanna Gumpf sometimes has her team compare their current team stats with successful Irish teams of the past. They monitor and compare stats like batting averages, home runs, ERA, and fielding percentages with past Notre Dame teams. They look at the some of the most successful seasons put up by past teams and Coach Gumpf challenges the current team to surpass their numbers.

Benchmarking against past teams focuses your current team on the kinds of goals and productivity they will need to achieve—plus gives them incentive to shoot for bragging rights over teams from the past.

The benchmarking idea works well if your program has a solid history of success and your current team is capable of achieving and surpassing past marks. However, it is not recommended if your program doesn't have much of a history of success—or you are in a rebuilding year with little chance of challenging the stats of past teams.

12. ANSON DORRANCE'S COMPETITIVE MATRIX

The North Carolina women's soccer coaching staff has developed an intensive Competitive Matrix they use to chart the results of drills and contests. The Matrix charts about 20 different areas including fitness results, various skills tests, and results of 1 v. 1, 2 v. 2. and other scrimmage type contests. The results are put into a spreadsheet that is updated and posted daily at their practice field.

Charting the practices and posting the results provides athletes with objective feedback on where they stand in comparison to their teammates. It holds them accountable for their focus and actions from start to finish. They can't afford to take plays off because it will show up in the stats and rankings. Most athletes tend to excel in a feedback-rich environment—and are eager to improve upon their scores and rankings when they are visible and readily available. Obviously, you may not have the luxury of having a staff of managers to record virtually every move your athletes make. However, you too can at least have certain parts of your practices charted.

(The intricate details of Dorrance's program are beyond the scope of this *Drillbook* but you can get a detailed explanation of Carolina's Competitive Matrix and see actual charts and rankings they use in the book *The Vision of a Champion* by Anson Dorrance and Gloria Averbuch.)

13. PITT'S BATTLE OF THE PANTHERS

Pitt Director of Life Skills Penny Semaia knows how to harness the power of competitiveness. Semaia and fellow staff member Abbi Terveer have set up a positive competition between Pitt teams by keeping track of their community service hours.

Semaia and Terveer post frequent updates of the Life Skills standings that are eagerly anticipated by Pitt student-athletes. Each team gets credit for the number of community service hours they put in, study sessions they attend, and Leadership Academy workshops in which they participate. Semaia and Terveer divide the total number of hours by the number of student-athletes on the team to keep it fair.

The winning team is awarded at the end of the season. You too can work with your athletic director to track and reward the community service hours of the teams at your school. You can make it a positive competition between your teams and it will spur on a wealth of community service opportunities.

14. TEXAS FOOTBALL'S DEDICATION DAY

Each year Texas football coach Mack Brown selects a "Dedication Game"—a game where players dedicate their performance to a specific person. Coach Brown says, "The most important thing is to focus on something beyond the game and to realize that without that person, their lives would be different."

He typically picks a game when he thinks the team might be flat and would need to play with extra emotion and competitiveness. He does this because the players put added pressure on themselves to play well when they dedicate the game to a specific person. Coach Brown specifically chooses the Dedication Day because he doesn't want a let down during the season by his players overlooking an opponent.

The players typically select their person for Dedication Day on the Thursday before the designated game. They then break up into their position groups and voluntarily share with their teammates who they've selected to dedicate their performance to and why.

Each of the players also makes a phone call to their chosen Dedication Day individual before the game to let them know they are dedicating the game to them.

Coach Brown says, "The most important part about Dedication Day is that it gives all of us a chance to think about the people we need to be thankful for and to compete in their honor."

15. DUKE BASKETBALL'S SLAP THE FLOOR DEFENSE

During a Duke men's basketball game, you might occasionally see the entire team slap the basketball floor with both hands as the opposing team is bringing the ball up court. Just why do they do this?

Slapping the floor is a signal Duke uses to remind all the players that this is a critical possession where they must get a defensive stop. The Blue Devil players must lock in their focus, give maximum effort, and play intelligent defense to prevent their opponent from scoring or getting an offensive rebound on this play. The signal is a way of quickly raising the team's intensity and competitiveness to get a critical stop. Despite being physically tired late in the game, the Duke players typically gain a surge of defensive intensity after slapping the floor to make the defensive stop that helps them win the game.

Similarly, rival North Carolina coach Roy Williams calls these critical late-game defensive situations a "Must Stop" possession with his team. When his players hear the term "Must Stop" they know they must be at their competitive best.

At the start of the fourth quarter, some football players and their fans will hold up four fingers or shake their keys. This too symbolizes that the fourth quarter is a key point in winning the game and necessitates an extra amount of focus, intensity, and competitiveness to finish the game.

So, whether it is a physical symbol or verbal phrase, you too can create some kind of signal to your team that you need their maximum competitiveness at critical junctures of your competitions. Ideally, they would be giving you maximum intensity and focus throughout, but these special situations definitely call for an extra burst of it as they often decide the outcome of the competition.

16. COACH DAN GABLE'S ACCOUNTABILITY TEST

Before each match, legendary Iowa Wrestling coach Dan Gable had his wrestlers stand in front of the entire team and explain how they were going to wrestle their opponent in their upcoming match. It put the wrestler on the spot and held each of them accountable for their plan and their results.

Coach Gable allowed the other wrestlers the chance to ask questions to each wrestler like:

- What are his strengths?

- What are his weaknesses?

- How are you going to beat this guy?

This line of questioning is actually an excellent form of a Scouting Report. Each wrestler had to invest the time to analyze his opponent and develop an intelligent game plan for success. It had to be well thought out enough to pass the scrutiny of his coach and teammates.

Contributed by:

Wes Bruns, Cedar Rapids Prairie High School

17. MATCH PLAY AND BOARD GAME CHALLENGE

To enhance the competitiveness of our team, we devised a different game for the end of each practice and awarded points for 1st, 2nd and 3rd (sometimes it was just for 1st or 1st and 2nd). This was done from the first practice in January until about a week before our first tournament in March. A running point total was maintained and those players finishing in the top four earned a spot on the travel roster. This helped our golfers maintain their focus at the end of practice since there was something on the line. It showed them that every single day of practice counts.

With eight players on the team, we paired them up or divided them into two four-person teams, so they played some type of game or match against each other. With golf being an individual sport in which one is playing the course, we have also had them play match play head to head to enhance the competitive nature.

Since board games seem to bring out the "best" in people, we had a "practice" this spring where the team did nothing but play board games. This was done merely as a means to encourage their competitive spirit and have them enjoy competing in a relaxed atmosphere.

Contributed by:

Renee Slone, Women's Golf Coach, University of Illinois

18. GPA CHALLENGE

As a coach, I also want our student-athletes to compete for the best grades in the classroom. Therefore, we have a team GPA challenge each semester. I split our 16 players into two groups of 8, and try to make them as equal as possible based on academic history. When the fall semester grades come out, I figure out the cumulative GPA of Group A and Group B.

At the start of the following semester, the group with the lower fall semester combined GPA cooks dinner for the group with the higher GPA at one of our player's off campus apartments. It's a fun team bonding activity, which also brings competitiveness in another area of life.

Contributed by:

Matt Giufre, Head Women's Volleyball Coach, New PaltzState University of New York

19. HOUSES

When I used to teach Physical Education I utilized a house system whereby every student involved in Physical Education class was placed into a house. As I lived in Auburn, each house was named after an Auburn athlete. We had Bolton House (Ruthie Bolton), Barkley House (Charles Barkley), Gaines House (Rowdy Gaines) and Jackson House (Bo Jackson).

In the hallway by the gym we posted results for all competitive activities from the class. As an example, during our volleyball unit we would have a chart listing the results of the games for each grade level.

The Chart accomplished several objectives.

1. It developed an esprit de corps, whereby all grades became aware of each other, and older grades would look to encourage younger grades since their outcomes contributed success to the whole group. As results were kept for all activities, a House may not be good in one sport or contest, but may be better in something else and could still be in the hunt for the overall championship. Students could request or create a challenge event whereby they felt their House could improve their standings.

2. There was an overall improvement in school spirit.

3. Student leadership improved as older students took more of an interest in younger kids and actually started to teach them skills and tactics to improve.

4. Competitiveness improved as results were posted and kids wanted to do well and not disappoint others.

5. Creativity was developed as kids could design posters and team banners and other decorations for their House. Kids that were "non-athletes" could still be involved and contribute by utilizing their creative means in an artistic or musical fashion.

Contributed by:
Craig Kennedy, Assistant Coach, Troy Women's Basketball

20. NAILS AWARD FOR COMPETITIVENESS

You can create a simple award to acknowledge your toughest Competitor(s) on a regular basis. I created the Nails Award to reward the athlete who was mentally tough as nails on his/her team over the previous week. This could have been someone who went all out during practices, had a great competitive moment during a game, or someone who was battling hard through the rehab process. The award was voted on by the teammates and coaching staff on a weekly or bi-monthly basis.

The winner of the highly coveted award was acknowledged by receiving a simple nail; yet this nail symbolized so much more. Many of the athletes taped the nails on their lockers as a consistent reminder of what was expected and what they had accomplished. You too can create a similar award with your team to reward competitiveness.

21. CREATE CHALLENGE LADDERS

Create challenge ladders where teammates compete against each other in certain skills. Challenge ladders are common in the tennis world, where players challenge other players in an effort to move up to the top ranking of the ladder. Basketball coaches can use them for free throw contests or one on one competition. Golfers can challenge each other in putting contests from various lengths. You can create challenge ladders for virtually any skills associated with your sport.

To create your own Challenge Ladder, put all your athlete's names on the rungs of a ladder that is drawn on a sheet of paper. You can start off the ranking by picking them randomly out of a hat. Or if you have done previous contests, position your athletes from top to bottom on the ladder accordingly.

Athletes then can challenge their teammates who are higher on the ladder to matches or skills tests. Most challenge ladders have a certain range that challenges can be made. Depending on your roster size, a good rule of thumb is that the challenge range should be no more than 20% of the roster. So a team of 10 would have a challenge range of up to two spots above. A team of 15, three spots above, and a team of 20, up to four spots above, and so on.

If the higher position athlete wins the challenge, there is no change on the ladder. If the lower position athlete wins the match, they take the challenger's position and everyone else moves down one position.

The athlete who wins can continue to challenge up until they lose. The loser must accept a challenge from below.

This challenging environment teaches your athletes to continually strive to move up the ladder while at the same time being able to take on and conquer challenges from others beneath them. It also encourages your athletes to continually work hard and put in the time to climb the ladder of success. Finally, it allows athletes to get pushed by athletes who are roughly at their same level of ability—so most challenges are highly competitive.

You can either incorporate your Challenge Ladder as part of practice time or allow for certain days to be challenge days before or after practices. Either way, a Challenge Ladder will keep your practices interesting and encourage your athletes to compete.

22. WIN THE WARM-UP

To gain a competitive advantage even before the competition starts, UNC women's soccer coach Anson Dorrance always wants his team to "win" the warm-up. Winning the warm-up means having a team that is highly energized, focused, confident, and eager to play. Not only does focusing on winning the warm-up get his team mentally ready to play, a crisp and spirited warm-up can also be a very intimidating factor for the opponents.

Arizona softball coach Mike Candrea also emphasizes the importance of a good, crisp warm-up for his team. The Wildcats always take pride in having a solid warm-up with clean fielding, accurate throws, and a positive and aggressive mindset. Opposing teams are often so intimidated by the warm-up that many opposing coaches take their teams out to foul territory to talk with them during the warm-up so the players' backs are toward the field. The opposing coach wants to prevent their team from losing the game before it even starts by getting psyched out from watching Arizona win the warm-up.

You too can emphasize the importance of "winning the warm-up" with your team. It will prepare them to compete and send a message to your opponents that you are eager to play.

23. TRAINING WITH BIGGER, STRONGER, AND FASTER COMPETITION

If a kid wants to get better as an athlete, most parents rightfully tell him to play with the older kids of the neighborhood. The child certainly takes his lumps early on, but in the long run he learns how to adapt and compete with the older kids who play at a higher level.

The same holds true at all levels of sport. This is why many women's basketball teams recruit their own set of talented male practice players. Tennessee women's basketball coach Pat Summitt says, "It's my experience that people rise to the level of their own expectations and of the competition we seek out. For that reason our teams practice against male players almost every day. Day in and day out, they go up against men who outweigh them and who can outjump them."

The male practice players provide the women's team with the challenge of training against bigger, stronger, and faster competition. The male practice players become a valuable part of the team in pushing the women to get better. They are also some of the team's biggest fans throughout the year during the actual games.

You too can seek to practice against bigger, stronger, and faster competition whenever possible. Have your freshman team compete against the jayvee team whenever possible. Have your varsity team compete against an experienced men's or women's team from the local community. Many college teams will have former All-Americans and Olympians train with them so their athletes can compete against top-level competition.

Your team may not come out on top too often, but they will pick up a variety of new skills and insights on the game. Most importantly, they will have great competitive role models as well as the confidence they can compete with those who play at a higher level.

SECTION 3

RELENTLESS COMPETITOR ACTIVITIES FOR ALL SPORTS

24. Top Competitors List

25. Classy vs. Crass Competitor

26. Warrior Nicknames

27. Competitiveness Continuum

28. Rate Your Teammates on the Competitiveness Continuum™

29. Dominate Your Territory

30. Prized Possession

31. Motivational Movies

32. Motivational Themes

33. Post-Competition Competitive Analysis

34. 20 Questions Post-Competition

24. TOP COMPETITORS LIST

Ask your athletes to make a list of the absolute best Competitors they have ever seen. These could be professional athletes they have admired from afar, people they have played with, or people they have competed against.

Ask them to list specific characteristics and qualities of these Competitors.

■ How did they train?

■ How did they compete?

■ How did they handle adversity?

■ What motivated these Competitors?

Use the names and the characteristics your athletes generate to guide the discussion about what it means to be a Competitor.

Use a white board or flip chart to compile the responses and look for commonalities and themes. This exercise will help your athletes develop a common understanding and definition of what it means to be a Competitor.

25. CLASSY VS. CRASS COMPETITOR

As we discussed in *How to Develop Relentless Competitors*, Classy Competitors treat the game and their opponents with respect. They compete hard but do so within the rules and act with honor and integrity.

Crass Competitors look to win at all costs. They disrespect opponents, officials, fans, and sometimes their own coaches and teammates.

To help your athletes better understand the differences between a Classy Competitor and a Crass Competitor, have them think through, discuss, and possibly even act out how you would want them to respond in the following situations:

- Taunting from an opponent

- Playing in front of a heckling, obnoxious crowd

- Opponent who is giving cheap shots

- Poor call from an official

- Losing a hard fought competition

- Winning a hard fought competition

- Blowing out an opponent

- Getting blown out by an opponent

- Opponent getting injured during the competition

- Opponent who has fallen down—Do you help them up?

Use your athletes' ideas as a discussion about how you would like your team to handle these and any other competitive situations. By deciding your response ahead of time, you can help train your team to act in a classy manner in the heat of battle; even though it might be much easier to respond in a crass manner.

26. WARRIOR NICKNAMES

This activity is a good one for those athletes who are reluctant to compete for whatever reason. It also is a good one if you work with female athletes who don't feel as comfortable being fierce Competitors on the playing field.

For those who have athletes who are reluctant to be competitive, try giving your team Warrior Nicknames to use with each other during practices and competition. The Warrior Nicknames could be something like Xena or Helga for girls or Thor or Zeus for boys. (Simply look at any Roller Derby Roster of names and you will see much more aggressive pseudo-names than the ones the athletes have on their birth certificates.)

Or if you're athletes aren't into Warrior Nicknames, You can also call your athletes by the names of their favorite Competitors (Kobe, Serena, Favre, Jeter, Misty May, Mia, etc.)

Have your athletes participate in selecting the names and also describing the Warrior-like attributes that they will compete with when using the name. The Warrior Nicknames give athletes permission to be someone else when they are on the field as opposed to the more cordial and gentile person they may feel they need to be off of it.

They'll probably have some fun with it at first—but it will remind them that they can and should be much more aggressive and competitive when playing their athletic role. You can have shirts made for each player with their Competitor Nickname on the back.

Contributed by:

Shelley Johnson, Carolina Leadership Academy

27. COMPETITIVENESS CONTINUUM™ DISCUSSION

Have your athletes discuss what a hypothetical person would look like at each level of the Competitiveness Continuum.

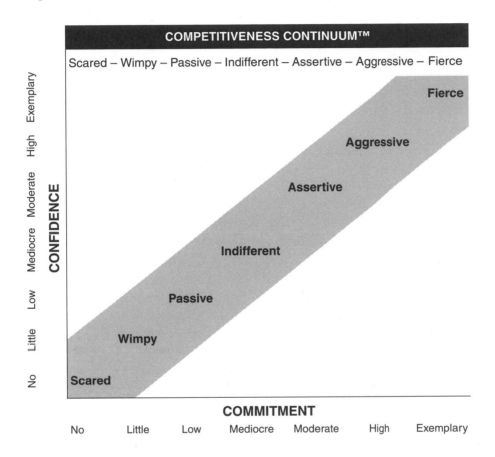

Competitiveness Continuum™

Scared—This is an athlete who fears competition and lets their opponent dominate the contest. They show no commitment, confidence, pride, passion, or persistence.

Wimpy—This athlete dislikes competition. Their opponent is the aggressor and dictates the contest. They show little commitment, confidence, pride, passion, and no persistence.

Passive—This athlete avoids competition and puts forth little if any effort to compete. Their opponent often determines the outcome of the contest. They have low commitment, confidence, pride, passion, and persistence.

Indifferent—This dispassionate athlete is pretty laid back when it comes to competition. They display mediocre levels of commitment, confidence, price, passion, and persistence.

Assertive—This athlete tries to compete and determine the contest but often with insufficient energy and determination. Moderate commitment, confidence, pride, passion, and low persistence.

Aggressive—This athlete seeks competition and looks to dictate the contest. They display high levels of commitment, confidence, pride, passion, and moderate persistence.

Fierce—This athlete loves competition and looks to dominate the contest whenever possible. They show exemplary levels of commitment, confidence, pride, passion, and persistence.

28. RATE YOUR TEAMMATES ON THE COMPETITIVENESS CONTINUUM™

Using the Competitiveness Continuum, invest the time to rate the competitiveness of each of the athletes in your program.

Coaches then can compile this information and share it privately with each individual on the team. You can have your athletes compare where they see themselves on the Competitiveness Continuum with where the team and coaching staff sees them.

If you have athletes who are ranked by teammates and coaches as being assertive or below, you can talk with them about some of the obstacles that might be keeping them from being more competitive. You can also use a variety of the activities, stories, and ideas in this Drillbook to help them bring out their competitiveness.

Scared	Wimpy	Passive	Indifferent	Assertive	Aggressive	Fierce
Names	Names	Names	Names	Names	Names	Names

29. DOMINATE YOUR TERRITORY

Some animals like lions, cougars, crocodiles, wolves, and dogs are highly territorial. This means that these animals fiercely defend and protect a certain area they consider their home and habitat. These territorial animals depend on this specific territory for food and to shelter their families and herd; so they mark it with their scent and protect it with all of their might. They know if they lose their territory to rival animals, they put themselves, their families, and the entire group at extreme risk of starvation and death, so they patrol and defend it vigorously.

In the world of athletics, there are also certain territories that are highly important to win, protect, and defend on the playing fields. The line of scrimmage is a specific area in football that must be controlled and dominated for a team to succeed. In soccer, players in certain positions must attack and dominate specific sections of the field to win the match. On the defensive end in basketball, guards must keep their opponents from driving into the lane while the post players must dominate the lane and, more specifically, the low block for the team to be successful.

Have your team think about the various critical territories of your sport, where key battles are won and lost. Ask them, "What are the specific territories we must not only protect but seek to dominate? Have them draw out these specific areas on a sheet of paper or white board.

Discuss the mindset and strategies your team will use to compete for and win these highly coveted territories over your rivals.

Further, have your athletes discuss the various positions and roles of your team. Based on your team's offensive and defensive philosophy, what specific territories are each of these positions in charge of protecting, winning, and dominating? Again, you can have your athletes draw the territories for clarity and significance.

Once your team and position players are clear about the specifics of their territories, discuss how you want them to mark, patrol, and dominate these areas much like a fierce predatory animal.

You might want to even do a little ceremony where each of your athletes actually walks the perimeter of their territory; much like a territorial animal would patrol it. Encourage them to make this territory their own and to take complete responsibility and ownership for it. Have them think about what is at stake for the entire team if they let a rival get the upper hand in their territory; your athletes must attack and/or defend it accordingly.

Remind them that winning and protecting these territories are vital to your team's health and survival, just like it is in the animal world. If your opponents invade and conquer these territories, your team will end up starving from a lack of respect, pride, and championships. But if your team dominates these territories, you get the spoils of victory.

30. PRIZED POSSESSION: WHAT'S WORTH FIGHTING FOR?

Objective

The purpose of this exercise is to help your athletes identify a prized possession they are willing to fight for at all costs.

Directions

Ask each of your athletes to bring in an object that is their most prized possession (or at least symbolizes it if they are reluctant to bring it in). Have them talk about why this prized possession is so important to them and what it means to them. (This exercise alone will give you great insights into your athletes as people and what is special to them. It will also be a good team building exercise, as teammates will learn more about each other. Be sure to have the coaching staff and any support staff involved with your team bring in an object too. If time is an issue, you could have 2-3 people talk each day and spread out the exercise over your pre-season.)

After each person discusses their most prized possession, ask them to imagine as if someone tried to take it away from them or destroy it. How would they react? What would they do to defend and protect it and why?

Most athletes would fight ferociously for the possession because it means so much to them. They are tightly connected to it in a way that they wouldn't want to give it up without a fight.

Ask them how this prized possession might relate to your team and its goals. What will they do when an opponent tries to take away the team's goals?

Hopefully your athletes are so connected to your team and its goals that they are willing to fight for them. Your athletes need to fight your opponents as if they were trying to take away each person's most prized possession.

During tournament time, you could talk with your captains about having each person turn in their most prized possession—then lock them up together as a team in a safe spot. Compete against your opponents as if they get to keep your most prized possessions if they win. This helps drive home the point that your opponents are trying to take something very valuable away from you. You can then give back each athlete's prized possession after your team has won the championship, or unfortunately if an opponent has won it.

31. MOTIVATIONAL MOVIES

With today's media generation, movies are a great way to communicate important messages on competitiveness to your athletes. Here are a variety of movies that you can watch to use as a foundation to discuss competition and competitiveness. (Obviously, invest the time to watch the movie before showing it to your team so that you can make sure the content is appropriate.)

Watching motivational moves together as a team can be an effective preseason or rainy day activity that you can use to explore competitiveness. Prime your athletes before the movie to be on the lookout for examples of competitiveness both in classy and crass ways.

Analyze what drives each of the Competitors in the movie… Is it pride, respect, status, approval, or a combination thereof?

■ How intelligently and intensely does each character compete?

■ How does each character handle adversity?

■ What kind of pride, passion, and persistence does each character demonstrate?

A League of their Own	*Hoosiers*
American Flyers	*Invincible*
Any Given Sunday	*Karate Kid*
Bend it Like Beckham	*Little Giants*
Braveheart	*Miracle*
Breaking Away	*Murderball*
Dare to Dream	*Navy SEALs: BUDs Class 234*
Days of Thunder	*Remember the Titans*
Dodgeball	*Rocky*
For the Love of the Game	*The Program*
Gladiator	*Youngblood*
Hoop Dreams	

32. MOTIVATIONAL THEMES

Developing a Motivational Theme for your team is a great way to create some fun and focus heading into the playoffs. Motivational themes help teams be inspired, competitive, confident, focused, and loose going into key tournament games.

The key to creating an effective theme is to find an analogy or story which best fits your particular situation. I've used a variety of themes with teams including Top Gun, Cross Country, Road Race, Pirates, and a Safari. You can then come up with little reminders of the theme to motivate your teams before games and keep them inspired during games.

Examples of Themes

Top Gun Theme—Locked on Target

Talk about playing like a jet fighter squadron. Need to be aggressive and tough while protecting each other. Relate different phases of an aerial attack to various team positions. You can get toy planes to symbolize your team and your opponents. Arizona softball coach Mike Candrea actually dressed up as a fighter pilot one year to reinforce the theme with the team.

Cross Country Car Race

Present the playoffs as a cross country road race. Each team is symbolized as a car. Emphasize the best car does not always win the race but the one that is best prepared. Get a Hot Wheels car to symbolize your team and one for your opponents. Smash your opponent's car when you get a win and start your own junkyard collection.

Green Berets

Players need to be mentally tough to handle any kind of situation. Green Berets are equipped for guerilla warfare and are good when your team is an underdog with an unconventional way.

Safari—Big Game Hunting

Emphasize the players need to be in an attack mode and the law of the jungle is "Survival of the Fittest." Each game is a "big game" and you must hunt down each opponent.

Pirate Theme

A pirate theme is great for a renegade, underdog team looking to steal away a championship from a highly ranked team. Get some pirate hats, bandanas, and a hook—and lead your team to the treasure.

33. POST-GAME COMPETITON ANALYSIS

You can use the questions below to help your team assess and analyze how well they competed following a game.

On a 1-10 scale, rate the following:

Purposeful

- ■ How passionate were we today? Did we have a clear and compelling reason for going to war?

Powerful

- ■ How well did we aggressively attack our opponents or game plan and how well did we dictate the tone and tempo of the competition?

Planned

- ■ How well did we devise an intelligent game plan that maximized our strengths and attacked our opponent's weaknesses?

Precise

- ■ How well did we execute our game plan, make adjustments, and stay focused on the task at hand?

Persistent

- ■ How well did we relentlessly persist and fight to the finish?

- ■ Did our competitiveness improve or subside at any points during the competition? If so, why?

- ■ How would you rate your own competitiveness today?

- ■ Who were the people who displayed the kind of competitiveness we are looking for on this team? What specifically did they do?

- ■ How would you rate the competitiveness of our opponents? What can we learn from them?

34. 20 POST-COMPETITION COMPETITIVENESS QUESTIONS

Use this sheet to help you, your staff, and team evaluate how well you competed.

How well did we:

1. Have a clear and compelling purpose for this competition ❑

2. Compete with pride, passion, and intensity ❑

3. Put in the quality preparation to fully prepare ourselves for the battle ❑

4. Assess, analyze, and attack the weaknesses of our opponent ❑

5. Neutralize or disable the strengths of our opponent ❑

6. Recognize and play to our strengths ❑

7. Demand a high level of investment and focus from our teammates ❑

8. Exert intense physical and mental effort throughout the battle ❑

9. Dictate the tempo and tone of the competition ❑

10. Dictate the tempo and tone of the competition ❑

11. Compete with confidence, trusting our preparation and plan ❑

12. Manage our emotions and not show any frustration or weakness ❑

13. Comeback time after time despite obstacles, adversity, and failure ❑

14. Make smart physical and tactical adjustments to outsmart our opponent ❑

15. Force the opponent to earn every success they got rather than handing it to them ❑

16. Breakdown, wear down, and outlast the opponent through a relentless effort ❑

17. Get stronger and more focused as the game went on ❑

18. Execute effectively during the late stages of the competition ❑

19. Refuse to lose and do everything ethically in our power to prevent it ❑

20. Represent ourselves and our team with pride and class (win or lose) ❑

SECTION 4

RELENTLESS COMPETITOR STORIES FOR ALL SPORTS

35. Old Coach and the Lake Story

36. Burn the Boats Story

37. Steel Mill Story

38. The Bike Story

39. Gila Monster Analogy

40. Finding Ways to Win with Two Kinds of Competitors

41. The Crying Scout Team Player Story

42. Lion and Gazelle Story

43. From Passive Freshman to Competitive National Team Captain

44. Mom and Baby Story

35. OLD COACH AND THE LAKE STORY

Former Colorado and Northwestern football coach Gary Barnett shared this story about competing and deciding to win in his book, *High Hopes:*

> *There was a high school team that practiced near a small lake. Across the lake lived Coach Jones, the winningest coach in the history of the state, and he was retired.*
>
> *Every day this high school team would come out and practice and practice hard, as hard as they could practice. But no matter how hard they practiced, they couldn't win. Every day, the retired coach would sit in his lawn chair and watch them.*
>
> *One day the quarterback of the team decided he was going to go talk to Coach Jones and ask him what he sees, why they can't win. So the quarterback went around the lake and said, 'Coach, I know you watch us practice every day. I know you know how hard we practice. I know you know how to win. Is there anything you can tell us that will help us win?'*
>
> *Coach Jones put his arm around the player and walked him near the edge of the lake. Suddenly, he grabbed the quarterback, thrust his head into the water, and held him down under the water . . .*
>
> *So the kid is about to drown, and Coach Jones pulls him up and says, 'When you want to win as much as you wanted that next breath, then that's when you'll win.'*
> *(p.127)*

Competitors make the decision to win as if their lives, or those closest to them, depended on it.

36. BURN THE BOATS STORY

In February 1519, Captain Hernando Cortes and his 500 men decided they were going to do something that no one else had been able to do in the last 600 years . . . Capture the world's most valuable treasure. Located in the Yucatan Peninsula in Mexico, the treasure contained the world's finest gold, silver, and rare jewels that had been hoarded by the same army for centuries. Many had desperately tried to seize it through the centuries but all of them had failed.

Cortes had heard about the treasure for some years and decided he was going to be the person to seize it. So he painstakingly selected men who were as passionate about getting the treasure as he was. After assembling his crew, Cortes and his men set out from Cuba to Mexico. They had 500 soldiers, 11 boats, and 16 horses; but they faced a formidable army of Mayans far greater than that.

When Cortes and his men reached the shore of the Yucatan Peninsula, they made their final preparations for battle. Expecting a rousing speech from their leader, the soldiers were shocked when Cortes ordered three short words... "Burn the Boats!"

Cortes commanded his crew to burn the boats they had just traveled in to get there. The soldiers thought he was crazy. His men said, "What do you mean burn the boats? How will we retreat safely if the Mayans overpower us? How will we ever get back home?"

Cortes told his men that now their only way home would be to capture the treasure and the city. If and when they did, they could then return home using the Mayans' boats.

With no option of retreat to fall back on, Cortes and his men stormed the city, seized the treasure, and returned home victorious. By not giving themselves any kind of out, they accomplished something that no other army had done 600 years previously.

You can share this story with your athletes and remind them of the slogan "Burn the Boats." Everyone must be 100% committed to success rather than having the option to retreat. You can even have special shirts made up with the slogan "Burn the Boats" on the back.

37. STEEL MILL STORY

Here is a great story about how steel magnate Charles Schwab helped to turn around an unproductive, struggling steel mill.

Here's the story as Schwab tells it in his book, *Succeeding with What You Have:*

> *I had a mill manager who was finely educated, thoroughly capable and master of every detail of the business. But he seemed unable to inspire his men to do their best. "How is it that a man as able as you," I asked him one day, "cannot make this mill turn out what it should?"*
>
> *"I don't know," he replied. "I have coaxed the men; I have pushed them, I have sworn at them. I have done everything in my power. Yet they will not produce." It was near the end of the day; in a few minutes the night force would come on duty. I turned to a workman who was standing beside one of the red-mouthed furnaces and asked him for a piece of chalk. "How many heats has your shift made today?" I queried.*
>
> *"Six," he replied. I chalked a big "6" on the floor, and then passed along without another word. When the night shift came in they saw the "6" and asked about it. "The big boss was in here today," said the day men. "He asked us how many heats we had made, and we told him six. He chalked it down."*
>
> *The next morning I passed through the same mill. I saw that the "6" had been rubbed out and a big "7" written instead. The night shift had announced itself. That night I went back. The "7" had been erased, and a "10" swaggered in its place. The day force recognized no superiors. Thus a fine competition was started, and it went on until this mill, formerly the poorest producer, was turning out more than any other mill in the plant.*
>
> *(Charles M. Schwab, Succeeding with What You Have [New York: Century Co., 1917], pp. 39-41)*

Without saying a word to the shift workers, Schwab tapped into his people's competitiveness by simply recording the shift's production and making it visible for all to see. In doing so, he created a healthy competition between the shifts to see which group could produce the best results. It's the same thing you want to accomplish within the individuals and sub-groups on your team.

38. THE BIKE STORY

The Bike Story is a great one when you have a team that needs to reconnect with their purpose and motivation for playing. It works especially well when you have an opponent who you perceive is trying to take something away from you.

This is a true story about a young boy who grew up several years ago in Louisville, Kentucky. The boy's family was poor and they couldn't afford much more than the roof over his head. However, the other boys in the neighborhood all had bikes except for this boy. He would try to hang out with his friends but they would go riding off and he just couldn't keep up with them.

Knowing his parents couldn't afford to buy him a bike, the boy decided to work for one himself. He found a job at a local grocery store and after about six months time, the boy finally saved up enough money to buy a second hand used bike. He proudly bought the bike, rode it home, and showed if off to all his friends. It was one of the best days of his life because he had worked so hard to earn the bike. He rode from dawn until dusk over the next few days.

Well, about a week after he bought it, the boy woke up one morning and went to his backyard where he had parked his bike. But it was gone!

He frantically asked all his friends, "Have you seen my bike?" He asked his neighbors, "Has anyone seen my bike? Unfortunately none of them had. The boy was devastated because someone had stolen the bike he had worked so hard for over the last six months.

A few years later, the boy got involved in the sport of boxing. To motivate himself before stepping into the ring, the young man would look over menacingly at his opponent and think to himself, "Hey, that's the guy who stole my bike!"

And Muhammed Ali went on to become one of the best boxers of all-time.

Author's Note: This story was used very successfully with the Arizona Softball team. They were heading into the NCAA Tournament in a funk and didn't seem to have the passion, focus, or determination necessary to advance very far. They had a national runner-up finish the year before to their hated rival UCLA. The team rallied around this story and theme, played with a sense of passion throughout the tournament, and decided that no one was going to take their bike from them without a battle. They went on to win the national championship.

39. GILA MONSTER ANALOGY

Here's a memorable analogy you can use with your athletes. It's about a real lizard found in the deserts of Arizona called the Gila Monster. Despite its small size, a Gila Monster bite is one of the worst a person can have. The Gila Monster is so tough that when it bites you, it won't let go. Although bites are rare, people often have to go to the Emergency Room to have the Gila Monster's jaws surgically removed from their bodies in order for it to let go. The Gila Monster's bite is relentless and extreme measures must be taken to extract it.

I've used this analogy with teams to remind them that their tenacity and competitiveness must be like that of a Gila Monster—something that their opponents think they will never let go or give up. (I have actually found some rubber Gila Monster replicas to help make the story more visual and the image stick.)

40. FINDING WAYS TO WIN WITH TWO KINDS OF COMPETITORS

Use this example to help your athletes understand that there are two ways that they can compete. Some Competitors have the sheer talent to take over games by themselves. More often though, most Competitors need to work through their teammates and get them to maximize their strengths so they can compete at a higher level.

North Carolina women's soccer coach Anson Dorrance divides Competitors into two camps when it comes time to taking full responsibility and leadership for the team's success.

1. The "Mia Hamm" Kind of Competitor

2. The "Carla Overbeck" Kind of Competitor

1. The "Mia Hamm" Kind of Competitor

Dorrance says, "There's the 'Mia Hamm' kind of competitor who basically says, 'Give me the ball, get out of my way, I'm going to stuff it in the back of the net, and we're going to win.'" These Competitors basically take the game over on their own and look to step up and get the job done at critical moments of the competition.

Similarly, basketball legend Michael Jordan used this same style for most of the early part of his career. Assistant Bulls basketball coach John Bach called this approach the "Archangel Offense." In the fourth quarter, they'd give the ball to Michael, tell everyone else to get the hell out of the way, and hope that Michael would save them.

Fortunately, because of their sheer talent and indomitable wills, Hamm and Jordan were both able to lead their teams to victory on numerous occasions simply by taking over on their own. However, 99% of athletes aren't as athletically gifted and physically superior to their competition as Hamm and Jordan were to simply take games over on their own. Which brings us to the second and more prevalent kind of competitor, the "Carla Overbeck" kind of competitor.

2. The "Carla Overbeck" Kind of Competitor

While talented, Carla Overbeck did not overwhelm and overcome the competition with sheer athleticism on the soccer field. Instead she focused on getting the absolute most out of her teammates. She invested time in getting to know them as people and players, and then organized them efficiently so that each of them could play to their strengths.

By getting her teammates to work together and play with confidence, whatever team Carla was on played up to their abilities. In this way, Carla competed by mobilizing and maximizing everyone's strengths. She organized and motivated her teammates in such a cohesive and competitive way that they would win.

Since you will be more likely to have more Carla Overbeck kind of athletes on your team than Mia Hamms, help them understand that they can best compete by working through others.

41. THE CRYING SCOUT TEAM PLAYER STORY

This is a story to use when you want to show your athletes about the emotional investment needed to be a Competitor as well as how Competitors take full responsibility for the outcome, even if they don't get to play in games.

Former Notre Dame football coach Lou Holtz once noticed a player still crying and inconsolable long after his team had just lost a crucial regular season game that kept them from competing for a national championship. Holtz was surprised because the crying kid was a freshman and scout team member who didn't even play in the game.

The player, Christopher Zorich, was upset because, as the scout team nose tackle, he felt he didn't do enough that week to prepare the Irish starters to win the game. He believed that part of the reason the team lost was on him. Holtz talked with his defensive coordinator about the kid who was so upset by the loss while the rest of the team went on their merry way, seemingly unaffected by the loss. Holtz said, "We've got to figure out a way to get that guy on the field."

Because of his passion and accountability, Zorich went on to start at Notre Dame, played a key role in Notre Dame's 1988 national championship season, was named the Lombardi Award winner as the nation's top lineman, and played professionally with the Chicago Bears and Washington Redskins.

42. LION AND GAZELLE STORY

This classic story is one that should get your team's competitive juices going whether your team is a lion or gazelle.

Every morning in Africa, a gazelle wakes up. It knows that it must outrun the fastest lion or it will be killed.

Every morning in Africa, a lion wakes up. It knows that it must outrun the slowest gazelle or it will starve.

The Moral of the Story: It does not matter whether you are a lion or gazelle. When the sun comes up, you had better be running.

Discussion

- Ask you team whether they think your team is the lion or gazelle—why?

- How is your team being chased today?

- What is your team pursuing today?

- What does it mean to "better be running" in terms of today's practice or workout?

43. FROM PASSIVE FRESHMAN TO COMPETITIVE NATIONAL TEAM CAPTAIN

How does a person go from a passive freshman to a competitive U.S. national team captain?

The transformational story of Carla (Werden) Overbeck is an inspiring one to share with your athletes.

During Carla's freshman soccer season at the University of North Carolina, Carla's name was continually at the bottom of the team's Competitive Cauldron rankings. She was passive and didn't win any 1 v. 1 duels against her teammates. She was overwhelmed and wasn't sure she belonged at a top-level program.

"I was not a naturally competitive person, but I learned a lot of my competitiveness in those drills (at UNC)," Overbeck says. "I was humiliated and knew that I had to get harder and tougher. As a player you want to have your teammates believe that you belong there. You want them to respect you."

So Carla made a decision and a commitment to compete. She worked harder and challenged her teammates in practices. She saw that by bringing confidence, toughness, and persistence to her workouts that she could breakthrough and move up in the rankings. By fully applying herself, she could compete with her teammates, gain their respect, and prove she belonged.

"By the end of my sophomore, junior and senior years, I loved the competition. It was all just about being comfortable with it," said Carla.

Carla's coach Anson Dorrance explains, "Somewhere between her freshman year and her senior year, Carla made a decision that it was OK to compete, it was OK to be the best. Her skills didn't get that much better between her freshman and senior years. What changed was her decision to win."

Carla played on four national championship teams at Carolina and became the U.S. National Team captain. She led the U.S. to Olympic gold and silver medals.

Discussion

- Ask your athletes about their decision to win. In what ways is being competitive a decision?

- Carla said she felt humiliated. How can you transform humiliation into motivation?

- How can you get your teammates to respect you and feel you belong?

- Have you made the decision that is OK to compete? That is OK to be the best?

44. MOM AND BABY STORY

Imagine a young mother sitting on a park bench watching her one year old daughter play on the playground. It's a beautiful sunny day and all seems well with the world. Suddenly, a strange man comes out from behind a tree, grabs the child against her will, and tries to run away quickly. What kind of response would you expect to see from the mother?

Almost assuredly she would become an instant Competitor! She would feel a burst of adrenalin and emotion and certainly fight for her child. No matter how meek and mild she might be during the day in most circumstances, a raging inferno of passion, intensity, focus, and persistence would burn inside of her to get her child back. She would let out a primal scream for help, chase down the abductor, physically confront and beat the living daylights out of him if necessary, and get her child back at all costs. She loves and values her own flesh and blood so much that she would willingly fight for her child against someone twice her size. Losing her child is just not an option.

While an extreme example, hopefully it is also one that demonstrates that virtually anyone, given the scary prospect of potentially losing something so near and dear to them, can almost instantly become a fierce and focused competitor.

Lying dormant within all of us is a ferocious Competitor. It awakens and kicks in when something that we perceive as very valuable to us is threatened or taken away. In the mother's case, the potential loss of her child kicked in her survival instincts to protect and fight for her child.

Discussion

- What is so precious to you that if someone threatened it our tried to take it away from you, that you too would fight for it?

- What are your opponents trying to take from you each time you compete?

- How will you respond?

SECTION 5

RELENTLESS COMPETITOR DRILLS FOR STRENGTH AND CONDITIONING

45. Wildcat Games

46. Monster Gators

47. Anson Dorrance's Speed Ladder

48. Superman Pushups

49. Running as a Reward—Positive Conditioning

50. Negative Split

45. WILDCAT GAMES

Developing Competitors has become a huge part of collegiate strength and conditioning. It is widely accepted, that all teams and athletes are lifting hard and running hard; thus they are getting bigger, stronger, and faster. Sure, there are different ways to get it all done, but in general, every elite level athlete and program is doing that part. So, the next things that we are all trying to get better at are nutrition and supplementation; and developing disciplined Competitors.

The athletes that we are dealing with at the college level have all of the skills, but they often times have succeeded because of their natural abilities. But, once they reach elite level play—they will succeed or fail based off their ability to compete and overcome adversity.

Wildcat Games

A few of things that I have found to be highly successful in developing the competitive edge are doing drills and exercises that develop a winner at the end—and then implementing the Wildcat Games.

The Wildcat Games are an offseason competition within the football team. In January, prior to starting the offseason workouts, the head coach and I select ten captains. Those ten captains then meet in a closed room and have a draft of "teams." They select their own team that will compete together versus the other 9 teams for the entire winter workout session and the summer workout session.

To draft properly, they have to understand what gains them points and what costs them points. In sports you often win or lose based off of how many mistakes you have in a game—so a huge piece of this is that when a player misses class, misses a tutor, wears the wrong gear, etc. he loses points for his team. (Very similar to a penalty on the field of play.) So, in the draft, the captains always start by taking the guys that will do it correctly first. Then they will pick those that will allow them to gain points.

Points are gained in the daily and weekly events. Within each workout on a daily basis they will compete with other teams and themselves to gain points. For example, on a bench press workout, we may finish the workout with a rep out test and if you improve your score you will earn your team points. It is amazing to see those players that will compete, and those that make excuses about injuries, etc. Some kids don't want to ever lose, and some fight and compete as seniors that wouldn't push that hard as freshmen. So, those type things happen on a daily basis.

Then, twice per week we have a Wildcat Games Event. All 10 kids of each team will compete versus the other teams in an event. It may be an obstacle course relay, it may be a van push relay, or it may be a wall sit competition. But all the events make them go very hard and earn the points. Then, at some point during the week, we will do agility stations and they do those with their team. If a player is slacking and not doing the drill correctly, he will get a demerit. At the end the team with the fewest demerits earns bonus points.

The events are worth winning. On a daily basis, if your team wins you may not have to condition, or you may get a special training table meal. At the end of the offseason workout—the winning team gets a gift pack from the equipment room that is well worth winning!!!

So, the "Games" are a huge part of our off season and we feel it really develops kids that compete; and it also shows us the kids that won't compete because of lack of interest; or simple lack of drive!!!

Contributed by:

Marc Hill, The University of Kentucky Strength and Conditioning

46. MONSTER GATORS

Set Up

Split the team into partners. Partners line up along the baseline. The first person in each partner group is at the line ready to run. The second person in each group is preparing to do wall taps with the ball. Each person will be doing 5 suicides (we call them Gators to remove the negative connotation).

Directions

- 1st person runs first Gator. Partner waiting does wall taps while she is running the Gator. (When her partner runs through the end line, the partner doing wall taps can begin to run her Gator.)

- 2nd person runs first Gator. 1st person does wall taps while she is running the Gator.

- 1st person runs 2nd Gator. 2nd person does wall sit with ball above head.

- 2nd person runs 2nd Gator. 1st person does wall sit with ball above head.

- 1st person runs 3rd Gator. 2nd person now does sit-ups.

- 2nd person runs 3rd Gator. 1st person now does sit-ups.

- 1st person runs fourth Gator. 2nd person does push-ups.

- 2nd person runs fourth Gator. 1st person does push-ups.

- 1st person runs fifth Gator. 2nd person jumps rope.

- 2nd person runs fifth Gator. 1st person jumps rope.

To increase competitiveness and mental toughness, we have the partner groups racing against each other. Be careful to monitor the players while doing their wall sits, pushups, situps, wall taps, and jump rope to make sure they are doing the exercises correctly.

Contributed by:

Kate Costanzo, Women's Basketball Coach, Allegheny College

47. ANSON DORRANCE'S SPEED LADDER

Directions

Rather than just ordering your athletes randomly when it comes to sprints, arrange your athletes in the order of how they finish each sprint and fitness test. The fastest finishers should be on one end and the slowest on the opposite end. The goal is to beat the people on the faster end of the line so that you can move up the line. Winners move up the speed ladder and losers move down.

This changing order keeps the intensity up for each rep. Athletes must look to beat the faster person on one side of them while not losing to the slower person on the other side of them.

48. SUPERMAN PUSH-UPS

Set Up

❏ Aerobic Steps

❏ Set up three aerobic steps about one yard apart as shown below. We use this set up so we can have four people going at once. Each player starts in a push-up position with their hands on the floor.

Directions

On the whistle, the athletes do a push-up and propel themselves up onto the aerobic step. They immediately do another push-up and explode themselves up in the air and land with their hands on the floor. This counts as one rep, and each player does as many as they can. After everyone has done as many as they can, we take an average total to determine which class (sophs, juniors, or seniors) has won.

Contributed by:

Terry Wilson, Chippewa Valley High School

49. RUNNING AS A REWARD—POSITIVE CONDITIONING

I inherited a team that had an interesting perspective on hard work and competition. For two years they had struggled and for some time they carried a roster of just 13 players. This created the idea that hard work and competition were negative concepts. They worked hard in games and still lost. Being on the bench wasn't a bad thing because you could rest; and with a squad of 13, rest was a luxury!

As a result we started using Positive Conditioning and saw an immediate change with our team. The concept is simple; anytime we do anything in practice with a winner and a loser it is the winners who run. If we play a small sided game the winners run. If we do relays the winners run extra. If we do a shooting contest the winners run we explained to our team that we want to coach winners. We want to coach people who will chase down a long ball with 30 seconds left of the clock. We want to have players who will do everything possible to win just one more game. We explained that we believed winners do not avoid hard work that winners simply work hard. This helped our players to see being on the field differently; they began to see it as a privilege, as something worth fighting for.

One of my favorite memories from the season is in regards to Positive Conditioning. It was a very hot September afternoon and we decided to end our practice with half field sprints. The last two people to cross the line were considered the losers and they were done but everyone else would run again. Our players did not want to finished last, they didn't want to be done, they wanted to stay on the field and every time we ran they fought harder and harder. When we got down to the last two people I thought we were done but both players stepped up to the line again, neither was going to stop until there was one clear winner. They had already done nine half-field sprints but they each wanted one more and their spirit of competition inspired us all.

This concept may sound simple because it is, but the rewards have been dramatic for us. It was a simple paradigm shift from seeing hard work as something negative to seeing it as something positive. I doubt the Mia Hamms, Abby Wambachs and Lori Chalupnys of the world are out working hard because they think they aren't fit or see themselves as losers. I believe they are out working hard because they are winners and they know winners do not avoid hard work, winners simply work hard. Positive Conditioning has helped our players to see themselves as winners too.

Contributed by:

Molly Grisham, Head Women's Soccer Coach, Wayne State College

50. NEGATIVE SPLIT

Objective

Foster competitive spirit while the athlete is fatigued.

Directions

Designed for long sprinters, middle distance, and or distance runners; "Negative split" is a designed run where the athlete goes out on a run at a specific pace (ex: 20 minutes at 6:00 mile pace) and then returns on the same route at yet a faster paced effort.

Discussion

The competitiveness comes in the ability to run faster on the return (when you are already fatigued) by the greatest margin possible. This helps directly to racing by being confident in knowing that you can always pick up the tempo in the later stages of a race effort (the weakness of most competitors).

Contributed by:

Lance Harter, University of Arkansas Track & Field

SECTION 6

RELENTLESS COMPETITOR DRILLS FOR BASKETBALL

51. Three Stops and Out

52. Master of the Boards—
    Michigan State Rebounding Drill

53. Four on Four Defensive Cut Throat

54. Sideline Passing

55. Gut Check Drill

51. THREE STOPS AND OUT

Objective
The goal is for a defensive team to compete and get three consecutive stops.
Can be played 3 on 3, 4 on 4, or 5 on 5 (half court)

Directions
Divide your team into 3 equal teams of 3-5 players each depending on your roster size. Make sure to have a good balance of guards and posts on each team.

Team A begins by playing defense against Team B, who starts with the ball at half court. If team A is able to stop Team B by getting a turnover or defensive rebound, Team A gets one defensive stop. Team A then takes on Team C, who again attacks from half court.

If Team A stops Team C by getting a defensive rebound or turnover, they would have two consecutive stops. Team B then tries to score a third time. If Team A can stop them again and get three consecutive stops, they get to stop playing defense and go to half court to get ready to play offense. Team B must go on defense to face Team C in an effort to get three consecutive stops. The game continues this way for roughly 15-20 minutes.

The number of defensive stops goes to zero any time the offense scores or gets an offensive rebound, or the defense commits a foul.

Use shot clocks in college. For high school, the offense must score or get an offensive rebound within 35 seconds or the possession is over and the defense gets credited with a stop.

Three Stops and Out games are always competitive, but they get extra intense when a defensive team has two consecutive stops. The defensive team gives maximum effort because they know how close they are to getting out of the drill and back on offense. Meanwhile, the offensive team knows they must score, get fouled, or get an offensive rebound, or they might find themselves playing defense for a long time.

Referee the games closely or loosely, depending on what you are emphasizing for that particular week.

You'll definitely see Competitors and leaders step up in this drill, especially when a team has been playing defense for a long time and can't seem to put together three consecutive stops. If a team can't get three consecutive stops, they might end up defending for the entire drill.

52. MASTER OF THE BOARDS—MICHIGAN STATE REBOUNDING DRILL

Set Up

❏ Master of the Boards is an aggressive rebounding and toughness drill. It is run 2 on 2 for 5 minutes at a time. Have players switch positions after 2.5 minutes.

Directions

Divide the team in half. Put one group on the baseline with the first two players lining up on the block. The second team should be out top with the first two players lining up on the elbows.

The coach has a ball near the free throw area and takes a shot. It doesn't matter if the coach makes the shot or misses; the players play the ball live and the first team that scores gets the point. There is no dribbling and no fouls are called.

After 5 minutes the team with the most points wins, and the losers run.

Teaching Points

- The players sprint to glass and rebound the ball and score quickly. The team on the lower block must chop their feet first correctly before the coach shoots, then quickly go find their man, hit him with a blockout, get their elbows/hands up, rebound chin the ball strong, and finish the play.

- The team on the elbows sprints to the rim with their hands up, tries to avoid the blockout, looks to rebound the ball, and score.

Contributed by:

Wes Bruns, Cedar Rapids Prairie High School citing Michigan State Basketball's Tom Izzo

Coach Tom Izzo's team's are known for being tough and competitive. Michigan State has the letters PP-TPW on their locker room wall. It stands for "Players Play—Tough Players Win." Coach Izzo says, "Mental toughness and physical toughness go together. If you look back, I don't know how many teams in the last five or six years have won the championship without being tough. . . . The strong survive."

53. FOUR ON FOUR DEFENSIVE CUT THROAT

Objective

First team to score 7 points. A team can score only by being on defense.

Scoring System

In cut throat, you only score while being on defense.

Offense

> 1. Made field goal → team goes on defense
>
> 2. Fouled in the act of shooting → team goes on defense
>
> 3. Two team fouls → team goes on defense

Defense

> 1. Rebound = 1 point
>
> 2. Turnover = 1 point

Divide team into 3 groups; two groups play while one group waits to come in at the baseline. The group waiting to come in must communicate match-ups for both possible opponents. A group always enters the drill on offense.

We observe no out of bounds in this drill . . . we play everything.

Coach's discretion on any jump ball situation; same two groups may replay or change of groups can be made.

Coach may specify a particular area of emphasis: contesting shots, blockouts, help-side stance, etc. The coach can make a lack of execution of one of these areas a turnover.

Contributed by:

Dean Lockwood, Tennessee Women's Basketball Assistant Coach

54. SIDELINE PASSING

Objective
The goal is for the players to make 85 layups in two minutes without the ball hitting the floor. (You can raise or lower the number of layups based on your team's ability.)

Set Up
The drill uses four basketballs. Start a player under each basket with a ball and position the rest of the players spaced out evenly along each sideline. The other two basketballs begin with the two players who are on the sideline at halfcourt.

Directions
The four balls are passed simultaneously around the perimeter of the court along the sidelines with players passing and cutting to the basket and making layups at breakneck speed.

The basketballs are passed down the sidelines from player to player. After passing the ball, the sideline players move up the sideline and take the place of the teammate they passed to. The last pass is made to the cutter who makes the layup. The last passer follows his pass to get the rebound. He then outlets the pass to the opposite sideline and sprints down the lane from one end of the court to the other as the ball is advanced along the sideline. He becomes the cutter and makes a layup. The drill should be done on both sides of the court with the players so the players can work on both right and left-handed layups.

This is a full court drill, pushing the players to exhaustion as they race against the clock making precise passes and making baskets in transition. Each basket the team makes over 85 earns them a "mulligan" when it's time for sprints. Each basket below 85 adds a sprint. An unintended benefit of challenging the kids to beat the clock is the fact that when we started doing this drill early in the season the goal was 75 layups. We ended the season by raising the goal to 85 with the team regularly making 86 and 87 layups.

Contributed by:
Waleed Samaha, Huron High School Basketball

55. GUT CHECK DRILL

Objective

This drill is great because it teaches our kids to compete in many different facets of the game.

Set Up

We start with one defender in a defensive help side position, usually in the middle of the lane, guarding a player on the wing with the ball on the opposite wing. We'll have two offensive players on the perimeter, one on each wing.

Directions

The offensive players will skip the ball on the perimeter. The defender must work on his defensive close outs on his man while sprinting to help side position when it gets skipped to the opposite wing. Once it gets skipped a couple times back to the player on the opposite wing, he will drive into the lane. It will be up to the defender to run to position to take a charge. A coach will be stationed under the basket and once the charge is taken, the coach will roll the ball somewhere in the half court and the defender has to run after it and dive on the floor to retrieve it.

We love this drill because it teaches help side defense, proper defensive rotation on the dribble drive, how to take a charge, getting up quickly to stay in a play, and diving on the floor after a loose ball—all things important to COMPETING!

Contributed by:

Rich Hoyt, Summit Country Day High School, Cincinnati, OH

SECTION 7

RELENTLESS COMPETITOR DRILLS FOR SOCCER

56. 4 v 4 + 2 Game

57. Dawg Bowl

58. Attitude Training

59. 3 v 2 + GK's

60. Deal With It

56. 4 V 4 + 2 GAME

Objective

This is an exercise based on soccer specific research from Europe. Their results showed that in general, the fittest teams are at the top of the European leagues. We make this exercise competitive by creating a tournament of 4 teams within the team. At the end of a round robin, we play a Toilet Bowl and a Super Bowl.

Set Up

4 v 4 + 2 Game (Can play 3 v 3 +1 or 5 v 5 + 2) Games played to Large Goals w/ GK's

Decide on field size based on numbers or aim of coach (larger field for more fitness, smaller field for technical work and speed of play). For 4 v 4 + 2 the field size is 75 yards long x 50 yards wide played cross field in one half of the field. A second game is played simultaneously in the other half of the field. The game must be continually played at a very high intensity so extra balls are placed at each goal and around the field . . . . No set plays are taken, restart every stoppage immediately.

Directions

4 v 4 + 2. Duration: 4 Minutes at the highest intensity possible. Heart Rate Monitors are worn and target heart rates are 170-190 bpm for college and adult players. Players have 4 minutes active rest. Get a quick drink and then do simple skill training at Heart Rate 120–140.

Scoring: A half line is created and all attackers must be across the half line for a goal to count as 1 point. If any attacker is not across the line, the goal does not count. If any defending player is not back in their own half when the attacking team scores, the goal counts 2 points. After the round robin, 1st and 2nd place teams play the championship game and 3rd and 4th play a consolation game.

Discussion

Players compete for Fitness Training Game Championship.

Multiple soccer benefits from playing the game, finishing, GK's dealing with lots of shots, etc. Transition to attack and defense is critical aspect of the game.

Aerobic Fitness is improved through playing soccer instead of running w/out the ball.

If you want to show your players how important fitness is in the soccer game, group them by fitness levels. Your fittest two teams should be in the championship game every time. The other players will be dying by the second and third games. To dramatically improve aerobic fitness, do at least 8 games in a row, 2x/week. The US Women did up to 12 games, 2x/week, in the aerobic fitness-building phase.

The players love these games as a substitute for running and got a lot of soccer benefits in addition to fitness. Competition was created by the tournament format.

Contributed by:

Greg Ryan, University of Michigan Women's Soccer Coach and Former US National Team Coach

57. DAWG BOWL

Objective

This series of games is to help players recognize the need to compete over time as well as recognize strengths and weaknesses in teammates.

Set Up

❏ Field is two 18 yard boxes.

Directions

4 vs 4 + Gks to big goals. For every goal you individually score you get a point. For every game you win you get 3 points.

We play at least once a week throughout off-season and also during pre-season as one of out "tests." Scores are posted…tends to reflect the pecking order of the team.

The three leading point getters act as captains for the final week's games. They meet before training and we hold a draft. The comments and choices of order are always confidential. The three teams then compete in a round robin before the top two teams compete for the championship. We have a huge Cup (known as the Dawg Bowl) that is awarded to the winning team, with the names of the winners engraved out the outside. It's a been a tradition here for over a decade.

Discussion

Each game provides coaches and teammates a chance to give feedback based on how the players competed each week.

Contributed by:

Jim Thomas, University of Washington Women's Assistant Soccer Coach

58. ATTITUDE TRAINING

Objective
This series of games is to help players recognize the need to compete as well as display competitive attitude and body language.

Set Up
❑ Part 1: 10-yard grid 4 players with a ball each.

❑ Part 2: Add four cones.

Directions
Part 1: 10-yard grid 4 players with a ball each. 1 defender who must win every ball in a specified time, e.g. 20 seconds. Each player becomes the defender. Times are kept for each defender; players do a "punishment" by order of finish.

Part 2: Similar to above but the balls are balanced on flat cones, now the players with the ball don't have the luxury of moving with the ball. They have to hold the defender off physically.

Discussion
Ask questions of players to help them understand that the result of the work they do or don't do has consequences. They are in charge of their own destiny.

In Part 2, athletes are forced to become more physical. Ask questions of them so that they begin to recognize the change in their physical behavior. Ask them to bring that physicality to every exercise.

Contributed by:
Brian Boswell of Ajax America (WPSL)

59. 3 v 2 + GK'S

Objective

To create an environment where lots of transition moments happen and players are rewarded for adjusting faster than the opponent.

Set Up

Game starts with 2 field players (2 red and 2 yellow) and a GK per a team on the pitch. Remaining players make a line off the pitch (one line per a color and the line starts in a wide of the 1/2 of the field that team is defending).

Directions

To start:

- Red GK serves to wide player.

- Red attacks as a group of 3.

- Yellow sends two defenders out to defend.

If shot is made:

- Red makes or misses a shot and all reds run off the field.

- Yellow two defenders stay to be joined by third yellow. Yellow counters.

If ball is stolen:

- Two yellow defenders joined by wide player.

- Red players leave except player who lost possession, one new defender on.

Discussion

I believe the game is a great teacher and players love to play! Every player wants to win and the drill/game has all the elements to compete and "shine" individually and collectively as part of a team. The core principles of the game are apparent and competitive, positive actions are rewarded in the pursuit of excellence. You have to be at your best in your moments on the field and that brings an inherent will to compete and mindset of focus, attitude, and belief and follow through, all qualities of a true competitor.

Contributed by:

Matt Potter, Washington State Women's Soccer Coach

60. DEAL WITH IT

Objective

To constantly put players in game-like scenarios so they have an opportunity to make mistakes and learn and grow from them prior to facing similar situations in competition. To teach players to have a competitive and "problem-solving-first" attitude given any scenario.

Set Up

Have popsicle sticks with game scenarios written on one end in a can (loaded face down). Game scenarios can be anything one might face in a game. Examples include:

- Your team is a man up.

- Your team is a man down.

- Your team loses a man 15 minutes into the game.

- Face a poor referee.

- Face double the set pieces (earned) against your team.

- There is a loud crowd and your team can't hear each other (therefore you are not allowed to verbally communicate).

- Your team has a 2-0 lead.

- Your team is down a goal.

- Your team must play low-pressure.

- Your team must play high-pressure.

Directions

Prior to playing any game with even numbers 5 v 5 or above the team captain draws a "Deal with it stick." Her team must then compete the same as the other team but they must make tactical decisions and adjust their style of play to overcome or maintain the situation they have been given.

Discussion

Coaches and teammates must be made aware of the scenario drawn. However, the opponent shouldn't know what scenario the other is facing until post-match. (Coaches should always try to match a team dealing with a goal up scenario with a team dealing with a goal down scenario).

Post Match: See if the opposing training team was able to tell what scenario the first team was dealing with. Have a discussion. Have the second team evaluate the first team's performance and attitude.

Discuss how well the second team was able to identify, adapt to, and take advantage of the tactics used by the first team.

Review some "What is important now?" concepts to remember when faced with the scenario again, either in practice or in a game. Expect and hold players accountable for making the adjustments in the future.

Contributed by:

Twila Kaufman, Pepperdine Women's Soccer Associate Head Coach

SECTION 8

RELENTLESS COMPETITOR DRILLS FOR VOLLEYBALL

61. Compensation

62. Two-Minute Drill

63. Timed Rage

64. You the Man

65. Hitter vs. Hitter

61. COMPENSATION

Objective

This 3 vs. 6 drill forces the team at a disadvantage to figure out how to score points to get out of the drill. The coach can control the intensity and difficulty of the drill by the type of ball they initiate to the team of 3. This drill not only trains physical and mental toughness, but also creativity. The drill does not end until the team of 3 reaches their goal.

Set Up

❏ 3 players on Side A and 6 players on Side B

Directions

For the 3 players on side A to get out of the drill they have to score 7 points against the full team of 6 with the last 2 points scored back to back. If at any point either side does not make an effort to play the ball, side A goes to 0. Any player on Side A can score and they can attack from anywhere along the net. The coach initiates the ball to side A with either a free ball toss (middle school level) or an attack (JV and above level). The coach can set the intensity of the drill by making the first ball more or less difficult to side A.

Contributed by:

Joe Sagula, Head Volleyball Coach,
University of North Carolina at Chapel Hill

62. TWO-MINUTE DRILL

Objective

Create some match-type pressure and anxiety.

Set Up

❏ 2 minutes go on the clock.

❏ Determine who will be receiving serve first, whoever that is will be the only side receiving serve for the entire 2 minutes. (For explanation purposes we will say that Side A will start serving to Side B.)

❏ Side B is the only side that can score points. Once the clock reaches 0:00, Side A will get a chance to receive serve.

Directions

Whenever Side B scores off the serve receive ball they get a point and will then receive serve again, it does not have to be a first ball kill, just need to win the rally.

If Side A wins the rally they will begin to get free balls from a coach, once this begins the clock starts.

The goal of Side A is to continue to get free balls and run the clock down to 0:00 with as few points as possible being scored by Side B.

Free balls will continue to be given to Side A until Side B wins a rally.

Once Side B wins a rally, the clock will stop and Side A will go back to serve again to Side B.

This will continue until the clock reaches 0:00. Once this happens, Side B will become the serving side and Side A will be the receiving side.

Contributed by:

Jason Allen, University of Iowa, citing Rey Bechard, University of Kansas

63. TIMED RAGE

Set Up
❏ Play is set up with 6 vs. 6 teams in a normal rotation.

Directions
Team 1 serves. If Team 1 wins the served ball, they do not get a point, but receive a tossed ball from the coach. If Team 1 wins the rally on the tossed ball, they get 1 point and another tossed ball. If Team 1 wins the second tossed ball, add 2 more points to the score and they get another tossed ball. If Team 1 wins the third tossed ball, they get 3 more points. In this scenario, Team 1 has 6 points already. Basically, each consecutive tossed ball is worth 1 more point than the previous one.

Once Team 2 stops Team 1, Team 2 serves for the chance to win the rally and receive tosses. Your team rotates every time they win the serve, just like a normal volleyball game. The actual served ball is never worth a point, just the opportunity to receive tosses. Once the non-serving team wins a rally (whether from first serve or one of the tosses), play is stopped and the non-serving team rotates and serves. Once a serve takes place, the first tossed ball is worth 1 point again.

We play this game for a set amount of time, not to a set score. In this game, one team learns to build momentum and pile on the points, while the other side is working on stopping a run and then starting one of their own. We usually play for 10 minutes, and each time, the winning team tries to best whatever the overall team high score happens to be.

Contributed by:
Matt Giufre, Head Women's Volleyball Coach, New Paltz State University of New York

64. YOU THE MAN

Set Up
❏ 6 v. 6 on volleyball court

Directions
The only one who can terminate the play is the designated player on each team. The other team can then plan to double or triple block that player. If someone other than the designated player terminates it is a point for the opposition. Whatever the penalty is, the designated player has double.

Contributed by:
Tracey Kornau, Lakota West High School, Physical Education, Women's Volleyball Coach

65. HITTER VS. HITTER

Set Up

Here's the set up: Two hitters get picked to go head to head. They play rock, paper, scissors to determine who will get first pick. The winner gets to choose—she can either get the first ball or she can choose one of her teammates. (They almost always choose first ball. The next pick is almost always for the best setter.) Then they go back and forth until they have selected teams, old school style.

Directions

The ball is initiated by a free ball toss. We play it out. After the rally ends we immediately toss another free ball to the side that won. We continue tossing free balls until one hitter is +5. To score, the hitter gets +1 for every kill, -1 for every error. (We do not go below zero.) After someone gets to +5 the losing team has to run. We usually also impose a time limit of 3 minutes. If neither hitter can get to +5 in three minutes then both teams run. The scores of each game are recorded in our team cauldron.

(This game can be played with or without a block.)

Discussion

■ Players who want to win will choose the best teams, not necessarily friends so this is a great way to break up cliques. It is also a great reality check for someone who doesn't always work hard and doesn't realize it. To be selected to play is an honor and carries with it the responsibility to perform.

■ This game rewards aggressive hitting and relentless defense. There is no block so hitters are very likely to swing away. Also, there is no block so our defense must be brave and go for it. If a player fails to go for it on defense the hitter can ask to have the player subbed out. The hitter does not get to choose who her replacement will be. This is very rare in our gym and so when it happens it is huge.

■ Even though it is hitter against hitter, everyone on the court will reap the reward or suffer the consequences so they are encouraged to play hard for each other.

■ The winning team gets the ball, which is a HUGE advantage, so even if you don't get a kill there is great incentive to play the rally all the way to the end.

■ It is extremely demanding physically. The players who are the most competitive do not realize they are tired until they step off of the court.

Contributed by:

Shannon Ellis, Seattle University Head Volleyball Coach

SECTION 9

RELENTLESS COMPETITOR DRILLS FOR SOFTBALL/BASEBALL

66. Competitive Bullpens

67. 4 Corner 3 in a Row

68. Stay Alive

69. Wall to Wall Softball

70. The Quick Pitch Bunting Drill

66. COMPETITIVE BULLPENS

This past year we did not have a definitive Friday night starter but had several candidates so we decided to play a tournament with our 6 pitching candidates in what we called competitive bullpens. Normally guys would work on their particular pitches during this time individually but this allowed for a competitive environment and better focus in our work.

We had tournament brackets and a 2 game elimination. The players in the tourney would match up against another teammate and compete in a bullpen session of roughly 50 pitches. Bob Keller and Mike Penn, two of my assistants, would judge the location of the pitches as well as grade them. If the pitch met their standard the pitcher was given a positive if not it was a negative.

Example:

Points: Highlighted areas are category wins.

- 1pt per category per inning except Execution % weighted at 2pts.

- Bonus points are 1pt for each occurrence in an inning.

- If go over 25 pitches in an inning subtract 1pt.

- If you want to penalize walks go ahead.

Burgoon			
	1	2	3
1st Pitch Strike %	1/4= 25%	2/3= 67%	3/3= 100%
1-1 War Win %	2/3= 67%	3/3= 100%	0-0= 0%
Overall Strike %	10/19= 53%	10/13= 77%	9/10= 90%
Overall Execution %	7/19= 37%	8/13 62%	7/10= 70%
1-2-3 Bonus	0	1	1
4 Pitches or Less Bonus	1	1	3
1	5	8	
Burgoon Total	**14**		

Sinnery			
	1	2	3
1st Pitch Strike %	2/3= 67%	5/6= 83%	2/3= 67%
1-1 War Win %	2/3= 67%	2/2= 100%	2/2= 100%
Overall Strike %	9/15= 60%	12/24= 50%	9/13= 69%
Overall Execution %	6/15= 40%	9/24= 38%	4/13= 31%
1-2-3 Bonus	1	0	1
4 Pitches or Less Bonus	0	2	2
5	3	4	
Sinnery Total	**12**		

Contributed by:

Rich Maloney, University of Michigan Baseball

67. 4 CORNER 3 IN A ROW

Directions

The athlete has to hit 3 solid line drives in a row from a corner of the strike zone. Once they hit 3 line drives consecutively they can move to another corner. If they hit 2 and then miss they have to start their count over for that corner.

If they are competing against themselves, they can keep track of how many swings it takes to complete each corner or how many swings it takes to finish all four corners.

If they are competing against other athletes, the winner is the person who hits 3 line drives in a row from all four corners first.

You could also play it where the hitter takes one swing at each corner and sees how many consecutive line drives they can hit while swinging at a different pitch location each time. If competing against other hitters, the first person to hit a specific number in a row is the winner.

Discussion

These drills can help the hitters understand how to control their internal focus. Are they focusing on execution or the self-imposed pressure to be perfect or the race to be first?

Frustration more than likely will become a part of this drill and the hitter must learn how to deal with it positively.

Contributed by:

Karen Linder, Head Softball Coach, Kent State

68. STAY ALIVE

Objective
This game is for training girls fast-pitch softball players, or boys baseball players to approach pressure-packed hitting situations with a relaxed and adventurous attitude.

Set Up
All players count off consecutively in a batting order that includes the full team. 5 batters are in the hitting area at all times (1 in the batter's box, and 4 preparing to hit).

Directions
The game starts with batter #1 getting into the batter's box. Each batter has one swing available to them. The batter must swing if the pitch is a strike. If the batter hits the ball fair they will be able to get up to the plate again when their # comes up. After hitting the ball fair, the hitter goes out in the field to field the other batters' hits. If the batter misses on their one swing, or takes a called strike, then they go out to the field, and they are eliminated from the batting order. Pitches can be delivered by a pitching machine, or a pitcher who throws strikes. For consistency, it is advisable that the pitcher throw the same pitch and same speed throughout the game.

   The players in the field who have been eliminated, can get back in the batting order if they catch a ball in the air before it hits the ground. This keeps the fielders engaged even if they have been eliminated from the batting order. Players should take positions in the field that are spread out in order to avoid contact with each other when fielding balls in the air. If a fielder makes any physical contact or interferes with another player fielding a ball in the air, the player initiating contact would be eliminated permanently for the rest of that game. The eliminated player would sit on the bench until the next game starts.

   Players have 10 seconds to get into the batter's box after the previous player leaves the box. If the batter is late, it is considered a missed ball and they are eliminated from the batting order. It is up to the players to keep track of the batting order and to be ready to hit when it is their turn. This keeps the game moving very fast with everyone focused. It creates high energy similar to a pressure situation in a game. If a batter gets in the box and hits out-of-order, they are eliminated from the batting order.

   If the players in the field are not chasing the ground balls, the coach can call a time out. The players in the field are told that the game will resume when all the balls have been retrieved and brought into the pitching area. The last hitter "staying alive" wins the game.

Discussion
Often a hitter will have two strikes in the count. It is important that the hitter at least make contact and hit the ball fair with the one remaining strike. If there are runners on base, contact is important to move the runners. The perceived pressure by a hitter in a

game can increase with two strikes. If a player can learn to become excited and expectant with two strikes, rather than feel increased tension, then they have a better chance of success. Players really enjoyed this game. It is very exciting and fast paced. It duplicates pressure hitting situations.

Contributed by:

Scott Chausse, Softball Coach

69. WALL TO WALL SOFTBALL

Set Up
❏ Gymnasium

Directions

Two teams start on each side of the gym. The idea of the game is to advance the softball from one end of the gym to the other. A teammate has to catch a thrown or rolled ball and touch the opposing team's wall without "traveling" or walking more that a step.

The game is fast-paced, each team has to advance the ball to each team's wall which they play defense on. The balls are thrown or bounced or rolled to other teammates, interceptions are allowed and the intercepting team now becomes the offensive team. If a ball is dropped by teammates, the ball immediately becomes the other team's ball. They can run anywhere on the court, position themselves but once the ball is caught they have to remain stationary and make a throw. Sometimes the throw angles simulate game like throws and the best part is if we play for 15 minutes they have conditioned at a rapid pace and are usually pretty winded.

Contributed by:

Mike Truncale, Newburgh Free Academy Softball Team, Newburgh NY

70. THE QUICK PITCH BUNTING DRILL

Objective

The idea is to create game-like pressure, while working on batters keeping a nice, still bat while bunting. Everyone is counting on YOU to get it done with limited opportunities.

Set Up

❏ 2 teams are made (can be picked by players or coach)

❏ Teams pick a representative or 2 (or coach can pick)

Directions

The team reps compete in Quick Pitch:

Using a pitching machine, a tosser will shoot 3-5 pitches in very quick succession

Batters will be scored on how many bunts they get down out of the 3-5 pitched (pop ups count as -2, pull backs on a ball count as 1, pull backs on a strike count as -1) the team with the lower score will run sprints or suicides.

Discussion

Contributed by:

Paul O'Brien, Shippensburg University Softball

RELENTLESS COMPETITOR DRILLS FOR FOOTBALL

71. Coach Jerry Kill's Warrior Elite Program

72. Coach Pete Carroll's Competition Tuesdays

73. Bermuda Triangle

74. Determination

75. Swiss Ball Sumo

71. COACH JERRY KILL'S WARRIOR ELITE PROGRAM

Here's an amazing team building, discipline, and competitiveness program used by Coach Jerry Kill and Northern Illinois football to forge a championship team in the offseason.

See how you might be able to adapt this concept to your team:

The Warrior Elite—The Forging of a Champion

1. Each player votes for five student-athletes who they consider leaders. The staff counts the votes and the top six are made platoon leaders.

2. Platoon leaders draft their teams.

3. Each team begins with 5000 points. Points can be earned or lost each week according to performance in the classroom, off-season training, and community service. If a team disputes points earned or deducted, the platoon leaders resolve it.

4. The top two teams at the beginning of spring practice have no conditioning (running) for four weeks.

5. The team that finishes last each week will have extra conditioning for each week they finish last. This is done in an attempt to prevent teams from giving up.

6. The team with the most points at the end of the semester is declared the winner. The winning team receives a plaque to be placed in the locker room and will be served a steak dinner for their first meal in fall camp.

The Warrior Elite—Point Values

Beginning point value in each Team's "Bank": 5,000

Deductions from Point Total

-Missed breakfast 200 pts

-Quit a workout early 50 pts

-Miss a workout 200 pts

-Missed workout due to injury 100 pts

-Improper workout attire 100 pts

-Short Study Table hours 50 pts per ½ hour

-Missed Tutor Session 200 pts

-Late for class (Tardies) 100 pts

-Missed class 200 pts

-Missed Rehab Appt. 200 pts

-Any Miscellaneous Tardies 100 pts

-D's on a 6/12-week grade report 50 pts

-F's on a 6/12-week grade report 100 pts

Additions to Point Total

+ Made Tutor session/appointments 50 pts

+ A's or B's on any 6/12-week grade report 50 pts

+ 0 absences AND 0 tardies on 6/12-week grade reports 50 pts

+ Extra Study Table hours 50 pts per extra ½ hour

+ Community Service hours 100 pts per hour

+ Greatest Weight Room Improvement by a team 1 pt per pound of max lift improvement

NOTE: Team Leaders will have the ability to speak to the head coach about the removal of a group member who is a detriment to his team's ability to compete for the overall team Championship. The head coach will have the final decision.

Removal of a chronic problem team member: 500 points

Special thanks to Coach Jerry Kill and Kristina Therriault for sharing the Warrior Elite program!

72. COACH PETE CARROLL'S COMPETITION TUESDAYS

As described in his book, *Win Forever*, former USC football coach Pete Carroll created special themes for various days of the week to help focus his team.

Monday = "Tell the Truth Monday"
The focus was on evaluating the previous week's game in an effort to learn and get better.

Tuesday = "Competition Tuesday"
The goal was to create highly competitive matchups between individuals and position groups. (More details below.)

Wednesday = "Turnover Wednesday"
Since turnovers often determine the outcome in football, the defense would win the day if they could create a fumble or interception. The offense would win if they could take care of the ball and avoid a turnover during practice.

Thursday = "No Repeat Thursday"
The players attempted to execute their plays and assignments flawlessly so that they wouldn't need to repeat any of them in practice.

Friday = "Review Friday"
Friday was the team's last chance to fine-tune the details and review the game plan before playing on Saturday.

The primary focus of Competition Tuesdays was to stoke the team's competitive fires. Coach Carroll and his staff intentionally put the players in situations to compete with each other throughout the practice. Coach Carroll would create "Matchups of the Day" by asking players who they wanted to go against in one-on-one drills; receivers would challenge cornerbacks, and defensive lineman would call out offensive tackles. Competition Tuesdays also featured a lot of plays were the first team offense matched up against the first team defense.

Interestingly, Carroll says he was strongly influenced by reading about Anson Dorrance's "Competitive Cauldron," which we have discussed in the *How to Develop Relentless Competitors* book.

Carroll writes in his book *Win Forever*, "I adopted Dorrance's approach for a number of reasons. As a motivational tool, it helped us make sure the players were practicing at a very high level. . . . During the team period, we would keep score in every way we could think of: first-and-ten situations, second-and-shorts, third-and-longs, and so on. . . . Bragging rights were a given, and the guys loved to get after one another."

73. BERMUDA TRIANGLE

Set Up

❏ 4 cones; 6 footballs. Make a 5 yard square with the cones (yes, the name says "triangle" but the drill is conducted in a square!). Arrange the players in a single file line outside of one of the cones (can accommodate anywhere from 6-16 players); Place 2 coaches or QB's on opposite sides of the square, each about 5 yards outside the line. This makes the QB's 15 yards apart and facing each other - 5 yard buffer, 5 yard box, 5 yard buffer.

Directions

The first 3 players in line go into the box (the Bermuda Triangle). The QB's alternate trying to complete passes to a player in the box. Players try to catch and control a pass, and try to keep other players from catching the passes through boxing out and batting down the throws. To escape from the Bermuda Triangle, a player must catch and control 3 passes. They call out their completion count, "One!" or "Two" or "Three and OUT!" with each catch. When a player makes his 3rd catch, he escapes and the next player in line jumps into the drill. Some players are in and out with their 3 catches in a matter of seconds. Others can be trapped in the Bermuda Triangle for several minutes before battling their way out.

Contributed by:

Eric M. Gobblo, Athletic Director, Trinity Episcopal School

74. DETERMINATION

Set Up

❏ You need 1 Pop Up Dummy for every 15 players on your team.

Directions

Our best and most competitive drill is one we call Determination. Organize the players in groups of three by size and ability.

When a group is called to go, two of the players act as blockers for a pop up dummy and the other player has to tackle the dummy. The two blockers must use legal blocking techniques. The drill goes until the person tackles the bag or her gives.

If someone gives up they have to run a lap around the field. In 10 years has a head high school coach I have maybe had 2 kids quit before getting to the bag...

The whole team gets into this cheering for their teammate, urging them on and not letting them give up. Rotate through the whole team as your players will be exhausted after doing this once. If you have a large team you can run two or more dummies at one time. Generally you want about five groups of three to a dummy.

Contributed by:

Jerome Learman, Lake Michigan Catholic High School Football

75. SWISS BALL SUMO

Set Up

- ❑ 1 Swiss/Physio exercise ball (large/medium size).
- ❑ 2 Football Helmets
- ❑ Wrestling Mat/Wrestling Room

Directions

Two athletes wrap their arms around the exercise ball facing each other. The athletes can stand or kneel while holding the ball. The object is to push your opponent out of the circle, pin them to the mat, or pull the ball from your opponent's grip. Most matches last less than one minute to 90 seconds.

Swiss Ball Sumo is really simple, yet competitive. We feel it is a great competitive and conditioning drill. Our kids love it and it gets the juices flowing during those long gray months.

Contributed by:

Tim Kuhn, Offensive Coordinator, Hazelwood West High School, MO

NOTES

Page 22: Anson Dorrance and Gloria Averbuch, *The Vision of a Champion*, (2002).

Page 50: Gary Barnett and Vahe Gregorian, *High Hopes*, (1996), p. 127.

Page 52: Charles M. Schwab, *Succeeding with What You Have*, (1917), pp. 39-41.

Page 110: Pete Carroll, *Win Forever*, (2010), p. 84.

PHOTO CREDITS

Page xii: Roy Williams courtesy of University of North Carolina Media Relations, photo credit Jeff Camarati.

Page 3: UNC Football courtesy of University of North Carolina Media Relations.

Page 4: Lindsay Tarpley courtesy of University of North Carolina Media Relations, photo credit Jeff Camarati.

Page 16: Red Berenson courtesy of University of Michigan Media Relations.

Page 34: Megan Fudge courtesy of University of Illinois Media Relations.

Page 48: Rachel Dawson courtesy of University of North Carolina Media Relations, photo credit Jeff Camarati.

Page 60: CeCe Marizu courtesy of University of Illinois Media Relations.

Page 69: Michael Garcia courtesy of Stanford Media Relations.

Page 70: Marcus Ginyard courtesy of University of North Carolina Media Relations, photo credit Jeff Camarati.

Page 77: Erica Prosser courtesy of Lehigh Athletics Media Relations.

Page 78: Danny Gray courtesy of University of Michigan Media Relations.

Page 87: Amanda Waugh courtesy of Bob Twidle.

Page 88: Lindsey Berg courtesy of USA Volleyball.

Page 94: Lindsey Berg courtesy of USA Volleyball.

Page 95: Julie Sterrett courtesy of Lehigh Athletics Media Relations.

Page 105: Jennie Finch courtesy of University of Arizona Media Relations.

Page 106: J Lehman courtesy of University of Illinois Media Relations.

SALSC

Catalyzing and Connecting Student-Athletes
Who Want to Change the World

Student-Athletes Leading Social Change (SALSC)

A portion of the proceeds from this book will go to support Student-Athletes Leading Social Change (SALSC), a 501(c)(3) non-profit organization. SALSC's mission is to catalyze and connect student-athletes who want to change to the world.

What is Student-Athletes Leading Social Change (SALSC)?

SALSC is a passionate coalition of current and former college student-athletes who want to use their leadership skills to make a real difference on a local, national, and international level.

Why SALSC?

Many student-athletes have a deep desire to be involved in local, national, and international social change projects/organizations, yet rarely have the opportunity because of their demanding schedules. SALSC recognizes this fact and provides interested student-athletes with the support and flexibility to pursue their passions/interests while respecting their rigorous academic and athletic schedules.

To learn more about SALSC, visit our website at www.salsc.org

ABOUT THE AUTHOR

Widely considered the world's top expert on sports leadership, Jeff Janssen, M.S. helps coaches and athletes become world-class leaders in athletics, academics, and life. He is the chief architect of comprehensive and cutting edge Leadership Academies for college athletic departments at North Carolina, Michigan, Notre Dame, Illinois, Pitt, Georgetown, Arkansas, Lehigh, Colgate, and Houston.

Janssen also is the co-founder and Executive Director of Student-Athletes Leading Social Change (SALSC), a non-profit organization that catalyzes and connects current and former college student-athletes who want to change the world (www.salsc.org).

A prolific writer, Janssen is the author of several books, articles, videos, and websites on peak performance, team building, and leadership. His groundbreaking books *How to Develop Relentless Competitors*, *The Team Captain's Leadership Manual*, *Championship Team Building*, *The Seven Secrets of Successful Coaches*, *The Mental Makings of Champions*, and the *Peak Performance Playbook* have received rave reviews from coaches around the world. He also provides cutting edge content for coaches and captains on his two websites: www.ChampionshipCoachesNetwork.com and www.TeamCaptainNetwork.com

Jeff lives in the Raleigh/Durham area in Cary, NC with his lovely wife Kristi. They have a son Ryan and daughter Jillian. The Janssens enjoy spending quality time with family, traveling, eating at great restaurants, reading, and playing and watching sports of all kind.

For more information on Jeff's resources and programs, visit:
www.jeffjanssen.com
www.ChampionshipCoachesNetwork.com
www.TeamCaptainsNetwork.com